Color by Number

Color by Number

Understanding Racism Through Facts and Stats on Children

ART MUNIN

Foreword by Tim Wise

STERLING, VIRGINIA

COPYRIGHT © 2012 BY STYLUS PUBLISHING, LLC.

Published by Stylus Publishing, LLC
22883 Quicksilver Drive
Sterling, Virginia 20166-2102

Library of Congress Cataloging-in-Publication Data

Munin, Arthur Carl, 1977–
    Color by number : understanding racism through facts and stats on children /
Arthur Carl Munin. — 1st ed.
        p.   cm.
        Includes bibliographical references and index.
        ISBN 978-1-57922-635-0 (alk. paper) — ISBN 978-1-57922-636-7 (pbk. : alk. paper) —
    ISBN 978-1-57922-637-4 (library networkable e-ed.) — ISBN 978-1-57922-638-1
    (consumer e-ed.)
        1. African American children—Statistics.   2. Racism—United States.   I. Title.
    E185.86.M947   2012
    305.23089'96073—dc23

                                                            2012002065

13-digit ISBN: 978-1-57922-635-0 (cloth)
13-digit ISBN: 978-1-57922-636-7 (paper)
13-digit ISBN: 978-1-57922-637-4 (library networkable e-edition)
13-digit ISBN: 978-1-57922-638-1 (consumer e-edition)

Printed in the United States of America

All first editions printed on acid-free paper
that meets the American National Standards Institute
Z39-48 Standard.

Bulk Purchases
Quantity discounts are available for use
in workshops and for staff development.
Call 1-800-232-0223

First Edition, 2012

10 9 8 7 6 5 4 3 2 1

To Heidi . . .
there is no way any of this would be possible without you.

Contents

Acknowledgments

I am deeply indebted to the assistance of several people who helped make this book a reality. My sincerest gratitude goes to Rob Babcock, Vijay Pendakur, Evelina Ayrapetyan, Vanessa Stewart, and John Dugan.

Finally, those who know me well understand that community is incredibly important to me. In no particular order, I thank all of those who have added to my life and continue to give me energy. Thank you to my parents, Tammi, Nick, Maggie, Lenny, Jo, Jonathan, Sophie, Mark, Amy, Paula, Elisabeth, Greg MacVarish, the entire Dean of Students Office and Division of Student Affairs at DePaul University, Sumun Pendakur, Mike O'Sullivan, Georgianna and Marcos Torres Reyes, Carl Gustafson, Becky Seibel, Katie Van Tiem, Casey Bowles, the Wolf Pack, Bridget and Rob Kelly, Maggie and Karl Nass, Faith Morgan, Eddie Moore Jr., Timothy Spraggins, Susan Komives, Kimberly Moffitt, and Suzette Speight.

Foreword

I'M NOT SURE THAT THE AUTHOR OF THIS VOLUME would want me to say this, seeing as how my purpose here is to give a hearty recommendation to his book— a book about numbers, about statistics, and about how to understand them in relation to the issue of racial inequality. But in any event, here it is: I very nearly failed my only class in statistics during my sophomore year of college. It wasn't that I couldn't have done better than the D minus I managed to acquire. I could have. But at the time, I didn't see the point. I was one of those people (perhaps you're one, too?) who didn't understand how math, how numbers, how data, could possibly matter to my life.

Interestingly, I was already focused on the other, and main, subject of this volume: racism. I was a campus activist around matters of racial justice, in fact. But when it came to understanding the numbers that really highlighted the extent of ongoing racial disparity in the United States, I presumed that it was sufficient to simply memorize a few of them, just in case I found myself in some kind of debate or something. I didn't, however, truly appreciate the importance of really understanding them, of understanding how numbers can sometimes mislead, or when used correctly, illuminate the stories, the anecdotes, the analyses around race with which I was far more comfortable. To me, numbers were helpful only for winning arguments, not for grasping at a deep and symbolic level the degree of injustice to which millions of people were still subjected.

It was only after I was out of school that I began to appreciate how important it was to really understand the statistics of stratification—the algebra of oppression, if you will—in order to be an effective advocate for social change. This was in large measure because I began to see how often and easily racists and other reactionaries opposed to racial equity misused data in the service of their political agendas. And I also couldn't help but notice how effective that misleading data often was with a public that, like me, hadn't paid enough attention in class to really understand what lay beneath them.

So, to have a work like this which takes as its central task educating a public awash with innumeracy—and especially when it comes to the application of numbers to difficult and contentious political and social issues—is a literary and ideological godsend. Although I doubt its contents will matter much to those with a firmly entrenched commitment to racist and reactionary ideologies (they will need their own epiphanies, the likes of which rarely emerge from the mere presentation of facts, no matter how impressively arrayed), to those with open minds and a quest for truth, these contents could make all the difference.

For those who haven't given much thought to race matters, this volume could serve as an inoculation against the twisted political siren song of the far-right, providing sufficient knowledge so as to weaken the appeal of those who would manipulate their racial fears, anxieties, and insecurities, or try to deny the reality of racial inequality so as to push a color-blind— and therefore injustice-blind—agenda. And for those already committed to racial equity and justice, the contents herein could be even more important, providing us with the factual information needed to go forth and mobilize others to the cause, not to mention reminding us of just how important is the task that lies ahead.

Although facts alone will never suffice to win the day for a more equitable America, there is little doubt that such a battle can never be won absent a clearheaded understanding of just how much work remains to be done. It is with that truism in mind that I welcome this addition to the literature already extant on race and racism. It is long overdue, and Art Munin has provided us a great service by way of its production.

Tim Wise
Author, *White Like Me: Reflections on*
Race from a Privileged Son and
Dear White America: Letter to a New Minority

Nashville, Tennessee
April, 2012

Setting the Stage

THIS IS NOT THE BOOK I WANTED TO WRITE, BUT one that is necessary. I believe racism exists as a chronic and pervasive facet of life, as a factor that privileges Whites while oppressing people of color, and as a definitive barrier to growth and advancement for all of society. However, it is a sad reality that diversity and social justice educators must still devote significant time and energy to proving racism exists. Since electing President Obama into the Oval Office, the idea of a postrace society has grown in popularity. The argument is that President Obama's success indicates that race is not the impediment to advancement it once was. This is false; the success of one man does not undo a system as historically entrenched as racism.

Racism touches every iota of our existence, covertly and overtly. It is normalized and woven into the fabric of our lives, so much so that it is difficult to envision life without it. This is why it is increasingly important to question, seek answers, and report the truth about racist practices in our society. That is the mission of this book. It is a manual for those who wish to educate about racism and advocate for change. However, to do this work, it is vital to be armed appropriately.

In an increasingly data-driven world, we are required to show proof that a problem exists before we can discuss a solution. Those in positions of power are often influenced by only one type of proof—quantitative. Or, in other words—"Show me the numbers!" Though statistics can clear pathways, open doors, and trigger conversations, in my experience, social justice advocates and diversity educators are not adept at deploying this type of information. Those of us who do this work, myself included, are more practiced at using the stories of real people to exemplify oppression or privilege. These stories bring racism to life and have the power to bring much-needed authenticity to discussion of this topic. But, however powerful, stories are no substitute for data.

To kick down the door for people who are skeptical about the effects of racism, educators must be knowledgeable about the underlying facts and stats. Without these data, it is too easy to dismiss the pursuit of social justice as the work of bleeding-heart liberals. Winston Churchill once said, "If you're not a liberal at twenty you have no heart, if you're not a conservative at forty you have no brain." The implication is that being liberal is fashionable when we are young and uninformed. At such a stage, we follow our hearts and passions and display the rebelliousness of youth. However, as we get older and learn how the world *really* works, it will become increasingly clear that the liberal agenda does not make sense. The conservatives are the ones who use the full power of their minds.

The presumption of Churchill's quote is that the liberal agenda for justice is devoid of facts and cannot be supported by rational arguments. This is, of course, untrue. I concede that liberals have not effectively used all the tools at our disposal. There are logical, fact-based arguments that prove the destructiveness of racism and its effect on society. These facts and stats are a powerful and necessary tool. Educators must teach in a way that best promotes student learning, not in the manner the teacher is most comfortable. This book compiles the objective facts and established statistics on racism to make evidence-based, research-driven arguments that illustrate its chronic and pervasive nature.

Part of the reason it has been difficult to use this information is because it is scattered everywhere. This is where the symbolism of *Color by Number* becomes clear. When I was younger I loved the "color by number" games in the comics section of the Sunday newspaper. The numbers were inside an assortment of adjoined geometrical shapes that appeared to be scattered randomly. However, among this confluence of shapes was a picture. My job was to color each number the appropriate color. I would make all the number ones purple and color the shapes with a number two in green. I did this until I filled every numbered field with the appropriate color, revealing the previously indecipherable picture. I would often try to guess what the picture would be, but I could only tell once I stood back to look at my completed handiwork.

Social justice work is very similar to this game in that it remains largely sequestered. We rarely bring together the diverse social justice research that has been done in fields including education, medicine, law, history, sociology, and psychology, and this prevents us from connecting the varying colors and shapes to see what greater image emerges. When taken together, this work provides a comprehensive picture of the centrality of race and the effects of racism throughout our society, whether in educational institutions, health-care organizations, or the criminal justice system. There is a plethora of misinformation attempting to debunk the arguments put forth in this book. As such, it is vital to draw together the research, facts, and statistics that illustrate the somber reality of being born a person of color in the United States.

The title of this book has a secondary meaning as well. Just as "color by number" activities are directed toward children, this book and the research that drives it focus on how racism affects children of color in the United States. Children are a protected class in society due to their innocence and powerlessness. Children have no say about where they are born, what school they will attend, whether they will receive a doctor's

treatment when sick, or what pollutants they will inhale or ingest. Children have few, if any, choices. Yet, we live by the myth of meritocracy in the United States, believing that every person's social location is a product of his or her work. To put it another way, "You get out what you put in." Is it fair to expect children to take responsibility for the circumstances of their lives? That is one of the major questions this book addresses.

We all bear responsibility for the racism children of color experience. The material that follows is a stark reminder that we are not in a meritocracy. People do not simply get what they earn or reap what they sow; we live in a plutocracy in which those at the bottom experience great challenges and difficulties, allowing for few successes. I say few because our capitalist system does enable some people with exceptional skills and pertinacity to succeed, disguising the underlying fact that there is little social mobility in the United States. This illusion enables those on top to look down on the lower classes and blame them for their lot in life. However, any success story is more akin to winning the lottery than simply to pulling up on some bootstraps.

The argument I put forth in this book is not the obvious one for me. My life's work is with adults—not children. Adults of color are trapped in the same system that grips their children. However, like a district attorney looking at a winnable case versus a morally justified one, sometimes we need to make the argument we can win as opposed to the argument we truly desire. With the United States deeply invested in the mythology of meritocracy, it is easy to dismiss justice arguments on behalf of adults. However, in the case of children, the meritocracy argument does not hold up. The research presented throughout this book strongly illustrates the chronic and pervasive racism that children of color face in their formative years, and the very negative effect it has on their lives.

How I Did It

For each chapter, I performed a multidisciplinary search of the relevant literature. For some chapters, such as "Preventing Medicine: Health-Care Access," much of the information came from medical journals. For others, such as "Criminals or Children?: Juvenile Justice," the research stemmed primarily from the legal field. For every subject, I was able to identify a plethora of data compiled by researchers in a wide range of disciplines, including psychology, sociology, and education. Regardless of the field from which the academic inquiry stemmed, the results were more similar than not. Finally, I've included data reported by various government agencies. To its credit, the U.S. government compiles an incredible amount of information and posts it freely on various websites.

I made every attempt to make this a truly contemporary review of the research for each subject. The search parameters were not to accept anything published before the year 2000. However, at times I violated this rule because some topics have not been subject to large amounts of research.

Another reason for setting the search parameters in this way was to account for the incredible lag time between conducting research and publishing. Under the best-case scenario, it may take researchers a year or more to collect data for a study. Conservatively, the writing process may take another year. It can then take another year or more for the research to appear in published form. It is not unusual for an article printed in the year 2000 to be the result of research collected in 1996, and there are cases when the data are even older.

BY THE NUMBERS

I have always found statistics to be far easier to comprehend than any other form of math. Statistics have a story associated with them. When I was younger and was given a generic algebra equation to solve, my first thought would be, "And why do I care?" The number I found seemed meaningless, with no obvious relationship to the real world against which I could test it. My academic work in statistics changed all of that. When looking at statistical data from a research project, I understood the *why* behind the numbers. When I found an answer to a statistics problem, I could look back at the story of the problem to see if it made any sense.

The research I collected for this book presented a wide variety of statistical measures. However, I purposefully used data that readers would intuitively understand and that did not require specialist knowledge. For instance, if an article presented a test score stating one group earned a 132 and another 154, that difference might be meaningful. But I often excluded such

cases because, unless you actually knew what the test measured and how those scores lined up against the whole population, they are useless. I could have gone into extensive detail in every one of these cases to analyze the meaning, but I feared such a step would drastically diminish the functionality and readability of this book. Instead, I chose to create easily decipherable tables and figures and clearly explain their meaning in the text. My hope is that this will allow readers to flip to any section of the book, look at a table or figure, and, by reading a short paragraph, know exactly what the data means. My only noteworthy departure resides in my coverage of standardized testing in schools in which I describe fully the nature and norms of those assessments. The types of statistics found in this book are described in the following paragraphs.

Percentages

Percentages are used as frequently as they are misinterpreted. They are numbers used to identify a proportion of a population (McCall, 1994). For instance, in 2008, the estimated population of the United States was 304,059,724 (U.S. Census Bureau, 2009). This large number tells us the size of this country, but does not describe the people. One descriptor that is often used is race; Table 1.1 includes the estimated raw numbers for racial groups in the United States as of 2008.

TABLE 1.1 United States Estimated Population Using Raw Numbers, 2008 (U.S. Census Bureau, 2009)	
	Total Population
White	199,491,458
Black	37,171,750
Hispanic	46,943,613
Asian	13,237,698
Bi/Multiracial	4,451,662
American Indian/Alaska Native	2,328,982
Native Hawaiian/Other Pacific Islander	434,561

These numbers tell a story about race in the United States, but they are difficult to understand. We can easily see that Whites constitute a larger share of the population, but it is more difficult to decipher their proportion in comparison to the whole country. The percentage breakdown in Table 1.2 makes these data much easier to manage.

TABLE 1.2	
United States Estimated Population Using Percentages, 2008 (U.S. Census Bureau, 2009)	
	Population Percentage
White	65.6%
Black	12.2%
Hispanic	15.4%
Asian	4.4%
Bi/Multiracial	1.5%
American Indian/Alaska Native	0.8%
Native Hawaiian/Other Pacific Islander	0.1%

These statistics are descriptive and useful. They describe the makeup of the country as it pertains to these groups without weighing us down with the large raw numbers for each population. Another way to view these data is a pie chart, as depicted in Figure 1.1.

Now that these percentages have given us a baseline understanding of a population under investigation, other percentages can tell a story. For instance, it was estimated in 2008 that the United States had 13,412,000 low-income families. Blacks constituted 22% of this population, Hispanics 30%, and Whites 42% (Simms, Fortuny, & Henderson, 2009). Merely glancing at these data, we can rightly infer that there are nearly twice as many Whites in low-income families than there are Blacks. If one were to stop at this deduction, one would be left with an incomplete, even misleading, impression. In the case of low-income families, there may be twice as many Whites as Blacks, but according to the U.S. Census Bureau data (2009), Whites constitute a much larger percentage of the overall population. Table 1.3 illuminates this discrepancy.

In an equitable society, if Whites constitute 65.6% of the total population, they should also make up 65.6% of those in the low-income bracket. But this

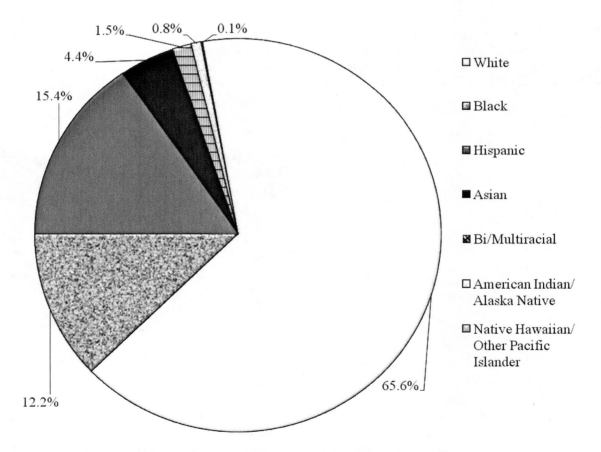

Figure 1.1   United States Estimated Population Using a Pie Chart, 2008

(U.S. Census Bureau, 2009)

TABLE 1.3
United States Low-Income Families and Race, Percentages
(Simms et al., 2009; U.S. Census Bureau, 2009)

	Percentage of Low-Income Families	*Percentage of U.S. Population*	*Proportional Difference*
White	42%	65.6%	−23.6%
Black	22%	12.2%	+9.8%
Hispanic	30%	15.4%	+14.6%

group is actually 23.6 percentage points lower in representation in the low-income family category. Conversely, Blacks make up a larger percentage than their overall size in the low-income population by 9.8 percentage points. The same is true for Hispanics, who constitute a greater share of the low-income group compared to their population size by 14.6 percentage points. The key word here is disproportionate. Whites are underrepresented while Blacks and Hispanics are overrepresented in low-income families, leading to a

disproportionate number of Blacks and Hispanics experiencing this social plight. Another way of representing this data is in a bar chart, as shown in Figure 1.2.

The innumerable discrepancies highlighted throughout this book provoke questions about how such disparity can even exist.

Correlations

A correlation is a statistic that "reflects the degree of relationship between two variables" (McCall, 1994,

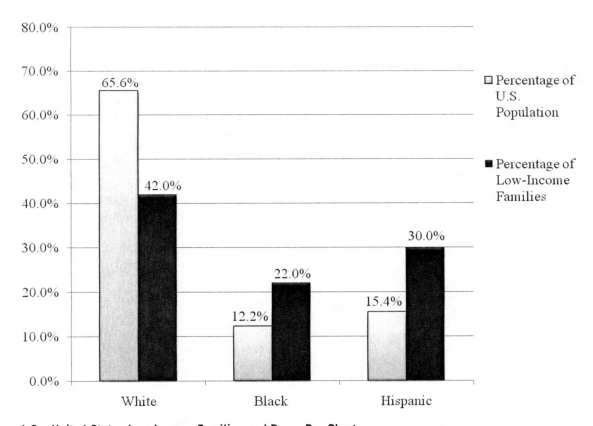

Figure 1.2   United States Low-Income Families and Race, Bar Chart

(Simms et al., 2009; U.S. Census Bureau, 2009)

p. 134). For instance, if a student spent one hour studying for a test and another student spent three hours, a natural assumption would be that the latter student would earn a higher grade on the exam. We would assume that time spent studying and test performance are positively correlated. As one factor rises, the other follows suit. As a factor decreases, the partnered factor lowers as well.

In instances of negative correlations, as one factor increases, a second factor decreases. An example of a negative correlation is video games and academic performance. As the hours of video games per day increase, there often is a decrease in a student's academic performance. This would make sense because the more time spent on video games means less time studying. The reverse is also true. If the amount of time spent playing video games decreases, then we probably would see a rise in the academic performance of the student.

In describing these two examples, I tried to be very careful in my use of language. I used phrases like "we would assume" and "we probably would see" to describe the correlative relationships. This is because of a vital mantra in correlations work: "Correlation does not imply causation" (Utts, 2004, p. 206). All a correlation can do is imply a relationship; we cannot guarantee this relationship exists.

Another important consideration is that not all correlations are equal. As seen in Figure 1.3, correlations range in strength from −1.0 to +1.0. A correlation of −1.0 would constitute a perfect negative correlation. Every single time one factor rises, another falls at a prescribed rate. A correlation of +1.0 infers the opposite. This is a perfect positive correlation whereby every time one factor rises, another factor rises at an even rate. Perfect correlations of either kind are never found. Instead, they serve as a benchmark for measuring strength. The closer a correlation gets to either pole, the stronger the correlation is (McCall, 1994).

For those correlations drawing closer to zero, or actually computed as zero, there is little evidence that the two factors are related at all (McCall, 1994).

Statistical Significance

This final statistical subject gives researchers the confidence to make assertions about a data set. "Statistical significance refers to the likelihood, or probability, that a statistic derived from a *sample* represents some genuine phenomenon in the *population* from which the sample was selected" (Urdan, 2005, p. 68; emphasis in the original). Like percentages, the best way to understand statistical significance is through an example. If we were attempting to examine a difference in car color preference between genders, it would surely be impossible to survey every single man and woman in the United States. However, statistics allow us to take a smaller sample to determine whether a difference exists. If there is indeed a difference, testing for statistical significance is what determines whether the smaller sample is actually representative.

Statistical significance, represented by a p-value, is an important standard by which we judge quantitative research. This p-value represents the likelihood that the present results are simply due to chance and do not reflect an actual difference in the greater population. The p-value often used to attest statistical significance in quantitative research is $p < .05$. This means that the probability of the results being influenced by chance is less than 5%. Researchers will, at times, attempt to make their results appear even more significant by reporting p-values of $p < .01$ or $p < .001$. These simply mean that the probability of results being created due to chance is less than 1% and less than 0.1%, respectively. One final reporting wrinkle are results detailed at $p \leq .05$. This is a slightly tweaked reporting mechanism stating that the likelihood of the results having been created by chance is less equal to 5% (McCall, 1994; Urdan, 2005).

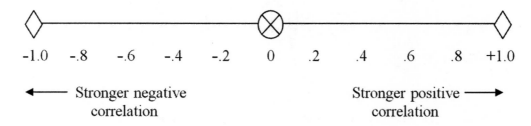

Figure 1.3   Correlation Range

There is one trap many beginners in statistics can fall into when discussing statistical significance. While a result reaching $p < .05$ is statistically significant, results that fail to cross this threshold are not insignificant. While they may not be worthy of grand extrapolations due to the amount of unaccounted error, the results can still be meaningful and used as additive information for the greater field of research.

THREE ISSUES

Three issues in this book must be highlighted. The first pertains to how complicated it is to discuss race. In this exploration, I can only report that the statistics published and the publications themselves are often incomplete and imperfect. As such, I have included plenty of numbers on African Americans/Blacks, quite a few statistics for Hispanics/Latina/os, several findings on Asians, and very little relating to Native Americans. Furthermore, bi/multiracial communities are excluded completely in the research. This is an unfortunate aspect of contemporary research as it exposes marginalization within marginalized communities. I believe many of my results pertaining to one disenfranchised group apply to others. However, as an academic, I know I cannot make that assumption without statistical evidence to prove it. Nevertheless, it does expose the need for more research, especially as it applies to Asians, Native Americans, and our growing bi/multiracial populations.

Exploring statistics for Hispanics or Latina/os introduces further racial complications. Technically, Hispanic is not a race; it is an ethnicity used to describe individuals descending from Spain or Spanish-speaking countries. Latinas or Latinos, herein after termed Latina/os, is a racial category used in the United States to categorize people from Latin America who often have brown skin. The majority of society does not understand the difference between these two terms and, consequently, uses them interchangeably. Nor do most people understand that it is possible to be both racially White and ethnically Hispanic. That is why on racial demographic forms you will often see White (non-Hispanic) or Black (non-Hispanic).

What this means for the current investigation is that all statistics reported for Whites and Blacks are derived from "non-Hispanic" categories. For statistics on Hispanics or Latina/os, I have simply reported what was in the research. I often use data sets for Hispanics, reporting on this group as a race alongside Asians and Blacks, even though the terminology is technically wrong.

As for the second issue in this work, we cannot explore race without an overlapping conversation about class. While these topics may covary, they are still completely separate constructs. The term I often use to describe class is socioeconomic status (SES). SES is a broad term used to describe the social class of a person "combining occupational status . . . income, education, housing and social status" (Annandale & Field, 2003, p. 48). A higher SES means one will have greater access to substantive commodities, such as money and health care, while also being able to take advantage of informal social connections. In the United States, race and class covary considerably, making it impossible to discuss one without the other. To demonstrate this point I present data pertaining to poverty broken up by race.

The poverty line for a family of four (two adults and two children) is $21,834 per year, and there is racial disparity in this population as depicted in Table 1.4.

TABLE 1.4 Families Below Poverty Line by Race (DeNavas-Walt, Proctor, & Smith, 2009)	
Population Percentage	
White	9.4%
Black	23.7%
Hispanic	22.3%
Asian	10.2%

White families constitute the smallest group, as only 9.4% live below the poverty line. Conversely, Black and Hispanic families are 23.7% and 22.3%, respectively. It can be argued that such a disparity constitutes a substantive class advantage for White families.

It is easy to translate these figures into an argument for how race and class covary. Families of color are much more likely to live in poverty and thereby have less access to societal benefits granted to the economically privileged. However, it is important to point out that this is not a perfect correlation. Not all people of color are poor, nor are all White people rich. It is very difficult to live in poverty, regardless of one's race. However, the research presented in this book, which investigates a broad range of societal issues, illustrates that access to entities such as higher income, health care, and education are much more likely to be withheld from children of color. SES is not a substitute for race, and it often complicates discussions about race and the effects of racism in the United States. Nevertheless, in comparing poor Whites to poor people of color, it is still better to be White.

The final issue is that, even as this book is printed, the data are aging. Researchers are continually publishing new findings on these topics. Therefore, it is important for readers to continue their study of these facts and stats. To assist in this undertaking, at the end of every chapter I have included a "Next Steps for the Reader" table, which provides information that will allow readers to continue their education in this area, and cites resources for locating the most up-to-date facts and stats.

ORGANIZATION OF THIS BOOK

The chapters of this book are not necessarily designed to build upon each other. They stand alone and can be read in any order. However, readers cannot comprehend the greater meaning and make important connections until they digest and reflect upon the sum total of this information. As the following chapters detail, the racism experienced by a child of color over his or her life course is substantial.

Chapter 2 highlights the racial disparity in health and health care in the United States. These negative health effects are exacerbated by exposure to pollution and other poisons, as covered in chapter 3. Chapter 4 moves into the legal world of juvenile justice, detailing disparate experiences within the juvenile corrections system. Chapter 5 covers the all-encompassing issues that surround primary and secondary education. This leads to chapter 6 describing the barriers to access and success in higher education for children of color. The concluding chapter provides greater meaning to all of the research findings, examines and problematizes who should take responsibility for the inequities that have been exposed, and calls on readers to become Social Change Agents within our locus of control.

REFERENCES

Annandale, E., & Field, D. (2003). Socio-economic inequalities in health. In S. Taylor & D. Field (Eds.), *Sociology of health and healthcare* (pp. 45–68). Malden, MA: Blackwell Publishing.

DeNavas-Walt, C., Proctor, B. D., & Smith, J. C. (2009). *Income, poverty, and health insurance coverage in the United States: 2008*. Washington DC: U.S. Census Bureau. Retrieved from http://www.census.gov/prod/2009pubs/p60-236.pdf

McCall, R. B. (1994). *Fundamental statistics for behavioral sciences* (6th ed.). Fort Worth, TX: Harcourt Brace.

Simms, M. C., Fortuny, K., & Henderson, E. (2009). *Racial and ethnic disparities among low-income families*. The Urban Institute. Retrieved from http://www.urban.org/url.cfm?ID=411936

Urdan, T. C. (2005). *Statistics in plain English*. Mahwah, NJ: Lawrence Erlbaum.

U.S. Census Bureau. (2009). Table 3: Annual estimates of the resident population by sex, race, and Hispanic origin for the United States: April 1, 2000, to July 1, 2008. Retrieved from http://www.census.gov/popest/national/asrh/NC-EST2008-srh.html

Utts, J. M. (2004). *Seeing through statistics*. Belmont, CA: Thompson Brooks/Cole.

2

Preventing Medicine
Health-Care Access

EVERYTHING STARTS WITH HEALTH. CHILDREN'S ability to leave home, walk down the street, attend school, play on the playground, do homework, and spend quality time with their families are all heavily influenced by health. If we are healthy, this goes unnoticed and *unquestioned*. It is not until our health is compromised that we become aware of the fragility of our bodies. This fragility is significantly affected by who we are, where we are born, and the color of our skin. As one author argues, "Health is produced . . . by the cumulative experience of social conditions over the course of one's life" (Daniels, 2001, p. 6). Our racist hierarchy has a major impact on the health of children of color in the United States, and access to adequate health care is a vital civil rights issue.

There is no better place in the United States to examine the racial disparity in health care than my hometown of Chicago. Chicago is known widely as "The City That Works." But for whom is Chicago working? The data in Figure 2.1 on 11- and 12-year-old Chicagoans answer that question clearly.

To be born Black or Hispanic drastically increases one's odds of having a lower quality of health. This affects home life, school, playing, socializing, and spending time with family. Debating health care for children is beyond politics, beyond a debate between socialized or market-driven medicine. Every child deserves a high quality of life.

There are many facets to consider when examining disparities in the health of children. To organize this complex topic, I first broadly describe the racism systemically affecting health care for children of color. This includes an examination of the current disparities in health-care access as well as inequitable health insurance coverage. From here, the chapter delves specifically into the topics of neonatal development and preventive medicine.

RACISM EXISTS IN THE HEALTH-CARE SYSTEM

Children of color have inadequate access to health care when compared to their White peers. The data also illustrate, however, that White children have unmet health-care needs, too. Fixing our health-care system does not mean increasing the number of unhealthy White children to equal the number of unhealthy children of color. Nor is the goal to decrease the number of children of color who are sick to the same level as that of White children. The only bar for success is ensuring that every child has access to immunizations, medicine, doctors, adequate nutrition, and health insurance. While the aim of this chapter is to explore the role that race plays in our health-care system, its underlying belief is that everyone deserves adequate health-care services.

Children of color frequently have untreated health issues due to inadequate access to health-care professionals. When comparing White and Hispanic

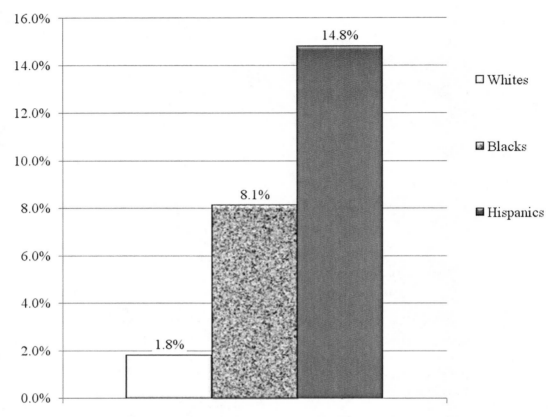

Figure 2.1   Chicago 11- and 12-Year-Old Children Reporting Fair/Poor Health

(Drukker, Buka, Kaplan, McKenzie, & Van Os, 2005)

children, there is a statistically significant difference ($p < .01$ in their unmet health-care needs: 7.1% of White children and 9.0% of Hispanic children reported unmet health-care needs (Newacheck, Hughes, Hung, Wong, & Stoddard, 2000). But race was not the only factor in the disparity. Children living near or at the poverty level were also three times more likely to have unmet health-care needs than their middle- and upper-class counterparts. Leaving health issues to fester is a dangerous practice as it "can adversely affect health status and functioning in the near and long term. For example, untreated physical, psychological, and behavioral problems put children at risk for developing lifelong chronic conditions" (Newacheck, Hughes et al., 2000, p. 989).

More evidence of the disparity between children of color and White children vis-à-vis health care was presented in the National Survey of Children With Special Health Care Needs. This study intentionally sampled children who already had a diagnosed health-care issue and needed health services. When comparing Hispanic and Black children with White children in Table 2.1, every statistic is significant ($p < .05$).

These numbers tell a story. Children of color are significantly less likely to have regular access to health care and less likely to have their own doctor than are White children. They also have trouble obtaining doctor referrals when they reach out for help.

I can still remember my childhood doctor and how comfortable I was with him. Our relationship was built over time, and I, without question, trusted his expertise. Far too many Hispanic and Black children never know that feeling, causing many to delay or forgo treatment. This can have a significant effect on a child's life. Of the children surveyed with special health-care needs, just under half had missed at least three days of school in the prior month. That can accumulate to more than a month of school missed in an academic

TABLE 2.1

Health-Care Access for Children With Special Needs
(Strickland, McPherson, Weissman, van Dyck, Huang, & Newacheck, 2004)

	Normative access to health care	*Report having their own doctor*	*Report having no issue in obtaining referrals to doctors*	*Delayed obtaining health care*	*Had health-care needs left untreated*
White Children	91.9%	90.4%	80.1%	8.83%	14.2%
Hispanic Children	85.2%	86.8%	68.9%	13.7%	21.9%
Black Children	88.0%	86.0%	76.2%	10.2%	21.3%

year. If you compound that reality over a child's entire academic career, you have a child who was never set up for success (Strickland et al., 2004).

A common converging factor in the research is the effect of SES. However, while SES is an important topic for consideration, it cannot undo the mitigating circumstances of racism. As evidenced in Figure 2.2, even when holding SES constant, Blacks and Hispanics whose SES was identical to Whites were still, by far, worse off (Weinick & Krauss, 2000).

One would have to double the percentage of Whites to have it equal the Hispanic population without access to usual sources of health care. In addition, the language barrier for many low-income Hispanic families increases the difficulty of accessing health care (Weinick & Krauss, 2000).

In order to understand this racial disparity in health care, it is necessary to move away from the general coverage on access to health services to specific examples of how race affects treatment. Kathleen Jablonski and

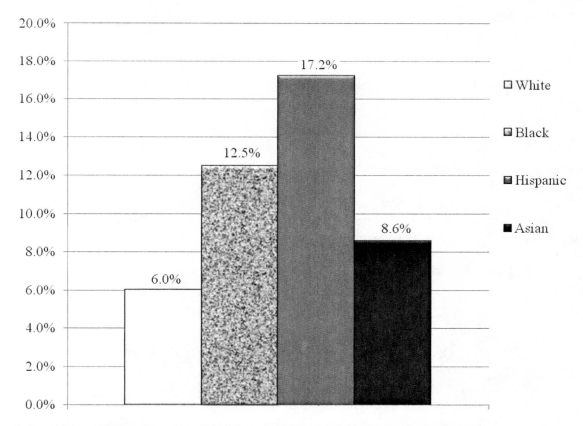

Figure 2.2   Children Without Access to Usual Sources of Health Care, SES Held Constant

(Weinick & Krauss, 2000)

Mark Guagliardo (2005) investigated a racial bias inflicted on children in the treatment of appendicitis. Appendicitis is a good medical issue to examine because there are no known racial or SES correlatives to its onset; it is easily diagnosed by a doctor; and there is often only one treatment, immediate surgery. Without surgery the appendix will burst and hurt organs, damage women's fertility, and even cause death. The study found clear racial discrimination in the treatment of this simple medical issue. When comparing other racial groups to White children, children of color were more likely to have a ruptured appendix, as illustrated in Table 2.2.

This higher rate of ruptured appendices in children of color also entails longer hospital stays and increased costs (see Table 2.3). All told, this reality meant a 175% longer stay in the hospital with a 97% increase in cost (Jablonski & Guagliardo, 2005).

This research clearly illustrates that when children of color have less access to health care, it has a direct effect on their ability to receive medical assistance at critical moments. And a primary reason for this inequitable access to health care is our failure as a society to provide health insurance for all people.

HEALTH INSURANCE

As reported by the Centers for Disease Control and Prevention (CDC), in 2008, 14.3% of the entire United States population lacked health insurance coverage. In delving deeper into this statistic, we find substantial racial disparity. When examining those without health insurance (those who were uninsured at least part of the past year and those who have been uninsured for longer than the present year), people of color in the total U.S. population carry an inequitable amount of this burden (Martinez & Cohen, 2008) (see Table 2.4).

TABLE 2.2
Race and Ruptured Appendix in Children
(Jablonski & Guagliardo, 2005)

	Ruptured Appendix
White	29%
Black	36%
Hispanic	36%
Asian	36%

TABLE 2.3
Ramifications of a Ruptured Appendix
(Jablonski & Guagliardo, 2005)

	Ruptured Appendix	Nonruptured Appendix
Average days in hospital	5.5	2.0
Average total cost of medical treatment	$17,905	$9,076

Hispanics are drastically more likely to lack health insurance at every level than are Whites. These full population numbers also translate into a similar disparity for children. Figure 2.3 reports that in 2008, 8.4% of all children lacked health insurance, another 12.9% were uninsured at some time in the past year, and 5.2% have lacked insurance for more than the current year.

These children come from all over the country. Reported in Figure 2.4 are the five states with the highest and lowest percentage of children who lack health insurance.

While these children may live anywhere in the country, their statistics mirror the entire population when it comes to racial disparity. As covered in Table 2.5, Hispanic children are nearly three times more likely to be uninsured than are White children (Children's Defense Fund, 2008).

TABLE 2.4
Access to Health Insurance, Total Population
(Martinez & Cohen, 2008)

	Hispanic	White	Black	Asian
Uninsured presently	31.3%	10.1%	16.3%	11.6%
Uninsured for part of year	35.4%	14.2%	20.4%	14.2%
Uninsured for more than present year	25.5%	7.0%	10.5%	8.1%

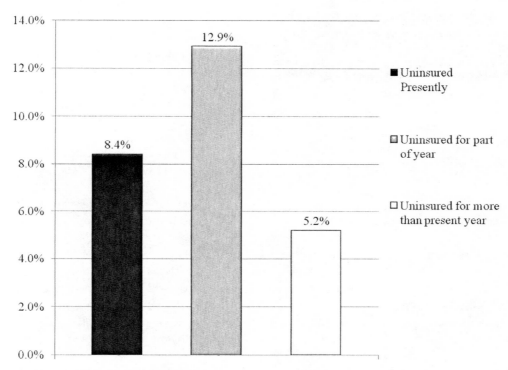

Figure 2.3   Health Insurance and Children, 2008

(Martinez & Cohen, 2008)

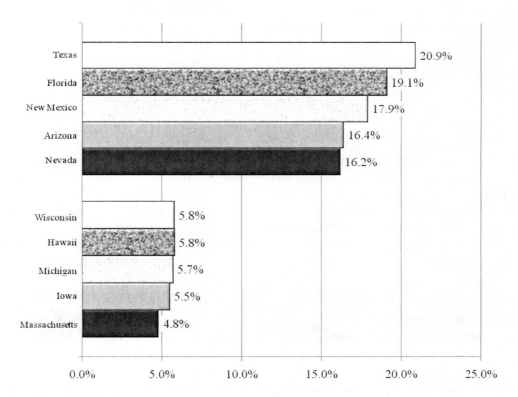

Figure 2.4   Top Five and Bottom Five States for Children Lacking Health Insurance

(Children's Defense Fund, 2008)

TABLE 2.5 Raw Numbers and Population Percentages for Children Without Health Insurance (Children's Defense Fund, 2008)		
	Total number of children without health insurance	*Percent of population*
American Indian	103,000	18.9%
Asian/Pacific Islander	379,000	11.6%
Black	1.5 million	12.8%
Hispanic	3.4 million	20.7%
White	3.4 million	7.5%

Aside from the sobering nature of this rampant racial inequity, there are two other findings to note. First, the Children's Defense Fund should be commended for including American Indians in its research and reporting. This population is ignored in nearly every study used in this book. Table 2.5 illustrates that 18.9% of American Indian children lack health insurance. With this number far outside the norm, we can assume this population is suffering in much the same way as other children of color. However, there are not sufficient data to support this assertion (Children's Defense Fund, 2008).

The second important takeaway resides in the gross numbers. A common argument invoked about these racial disparities is that, although children of color carry a higher percentage of negative social conditions, Whites account for a higher gross number. With Whites representing the overwhelming majority of the population, it makes perfect sense that their raw numbers would be higher in just about any category, including social inequality. However, even if I were to grant credence to this argument, it is thoroughly debunked by the data. When comparing uninsured White children to uninsured Hispanic children, both gross numbers are 3.4 million. However, as shown in Table 2.6, there were 44.7 million White children as opposed to 16.5 million Hispanic children (Children's Defense Fund, 2008).

Even though their uninsured gross number is equal, the ratio for the population is far from equitable because there are more White children than there are Hispanic children. A White child has a one in 13 chance of going uninsured, compared to a one in five chance for a Hispanic child. Even when those who would argue against the reality of racial disparity attempt to invoke an argument based on raw data, the numbers still reveal the role that race plays in health care.

This lack of health insurance coverage has a dramatic effect on meeting the health-care needs of children. One study focused solely on the health care of children who have special needs. Such children would include "those who have or are at increased risk for a chronic physical, developmental, behavioral or emotional condition and who also require health and related services of a type or amount beyond that required by children generally" (Newacheck, McManus, Fox, Hung, & Halfon, 2000, p. 760). These children are already predisposed to having health problems, which means the health care they receive is crucial. And yet, there is great inequity in the services these children can access.

Among the whole U.S. population, there are 12.5 million children with special health needs, 11.2% of whom have no health insurance. That is 1.3 million children with an enormous barrier between themselves and adequate health care. Those most likely to lack insurance were "older children, Hispanics, children from poor and near poor households . . . and children living in the South and West" (Newacheck, McManus et al., 2000, p. 761). The biggest discrepancy in coverage was for the poor and near-poor kids who were four times more likely to be uninsured ($p < .01$). This disparity is causing uninsured kids with special health needs to delay receiving care, as reported in Table 2.7.

Families with no insurance would like nothing better than to have their children receive the health care

TABLE 2.6 White Versus Hispanic Children Without Health Insurance (Children's Defense Fund, 2008)			
	Total number of children	*Total number of children without health insurance*	*Ratio*
Hispanic	16.5 million	3.4 million	1 in 5
White	44.7 million	3.4 million	1 in 13

TABLE 2.7
Health Insurance as a Variable for
Children With Special Health Needs
(Newacheck, McManus et al., 2000)

	Delay seeking treatment	*Unable to receive treatment*
Uninsured Children	19.0%	8.1%
Insured Children	4.0%	0.6%

they need, but the cost is too high. A total of 8.1% of families without health insurance coverage specifically cited an inability to pay as the reason their child did not receive needed health care. This is opposed to 0.6% of those with health insurance who failed to receive care due to cost. This is more than a 13-fold difference between these two populations (Newacheck, McManus et al., 2000).

Our government has not completely ignored this disparity and has attempted to alleviate this gap in health-care coverage for children. The most notable examples are Medicaid and the State Children's Health Insurance Program (SCHIP).

Medicaid was created in 1965 as a federal and state program to provide health care for citizens provided they met certain criteria. The federal government administered broad provisions for these criteria, but left the majority of definitions to each state. A few of the federal government stipulations are:

- Children under age 6 whose family income is at or below 133 percent of the federal poverty level (FPL)
- Pregnant women whose family income is below 133 percent of the FPL (services to these women are limited to those related to pregnancy, complications of pregnancy, delivery, and postpartum care)
- All children born after September 30, 1983, who are under age 19, in families with incomes at or below the FPL (U.S. Department of Health & Human Services, 2006)

States can apply for matching funds from the federal government for individuals not covered in the previously mentioned stipulations, such as:

- Infants up to age 1 and pregnant women not covered under the mandatory rules whose family income is no more than 185 percent of the FPL
- Children under age 21 who meet criteria more liberal than the Aid to Families With Dependent Children (AFDC) income and resources requirements
- "Optional targeted low-income children" included within the SCHIP established by the Balanced Budget Act (BBA) of 1997 (U.S. Department of Health & Human Services, 2006)

And while many of the requirements for this vital social program derive from income, the website providing the technical outline of Medicaid states clearly:

> Medicaid does not provide medical assistance for all poor persons. Even under the broadest provisions of the Federal statute (except for emergency services for certain persons), the Medicaid program does not provide health care services, even for very poor persons, unless they are in one of the designated eligibility groups. Low income is only one test for Medicaid eligibility. (U.S. Department of Health & Human Services, 2006)

Given that there are still many children in need of health care who are not covered by Medicaid, the federal government has also instituted the Children's Health Insurance Program (CHIP). This is referred to more commonly as the State Children's Health Insurance Program (SCHIP) since it is left largely up to all 50 states plus the District of Columbia to implement this service. This entitlement program was created in 1997 under President Clinton, but only became law because of the dedication of people like the late Senator Ted Kennedy and then-First Lady Hillary Rodham Clinton. SCHIP plugged many of the gaps left by Medicaid. Children meeting various criteria, most notably income-based, have wide access to health-care services, preventive medicine, and emergency care. The program has grown rapidly over the years and in 2009 was expanded to serve as many as 11 million children who lacked health care (U.S. Department of Health & Human Services, 2009).

Congress attempted to expand SCHIP, but President George W. Bush vetoed the legislation. This frustrated many fellow Republicans such as Senator Orrin Hatch of Utah who said that supporting SCHIP was "the morally right thing to do" and Senator Gordon Smith of Oregon who stated that President Bush was guilty of "an irresponsible use of the veto pen" (Stout, 2007). However, White House spokesperson Dana Perino stated that President Bush would not agree to expanding health care for children if the bill had "policies in it that should not be a part of the United States policy" (Welna, 2007). Starting in a starkly different direction, one of the first bills President Obama signed into law was the *Children's Health Insurance Program Reauthorization Act* (CHIPRA), which immediately increased health-care access for 4 million additional children while ensuring that funding remained stable for those already receiving coverage. After signing this bill President Obama stated:

> I refuse to accept that millions of our kids fail to reach their full potential because we fail to meet their basic needs. In a decent society, there are certain obligations that are not subject to trade-offs or negotiation—health care for our children is one of those obligations. (2009)

It is too soon to tell the effect this law will have on the lives of children without health insurance, but previous research on the effectiveness of Medicaid and SCHIP will be an instructive baseline for comparison.

Prior to implementation of SCHIP, the racial disparity in health care for children was statistically significant at every level. White children could consistently identify a primary source for health care, and they were able to keep most, if not all, medical appointments. As illustrated in Table 2.8, children of color, however, had the largest percentage of missed medical appointments and the largest percentage of doctor-recommended appointments that were never scheduled (Shone, Dick, Klein, Zwanziger, & Szilagyi, 2005).

It might seem easy to blame the parents of these children of color for their missed or never-scheduled appointments. However, if a family doesn't have the money to pay for health care, there is no decision to make (Newacheck, McManus et al., 2000). But with programs like SCHIP, some of the barriers to health care tumble down. Figure 2.5, a study of the New York SCHIP, highlights this reality.

All of these numbers are statistically significant ($p < .001$) and are representative of the power one social program can have. Prior to SCHIP in New York, 48% of children failed to show up for appointments with a primary health service provider. After implementation of SCHIP, that number plummeted to 4%. In identifying a primary health-care provider, keeping regular appointments, and gaining access to preventive medicine, the statistics all follow the same trend (Szilagyi et al., 2004). There are similar results in Colorado's Child Health Plus Plan (Kempe et al., 2005).

Another study evaluated some of the extraneous benefits New York SCHIP had for the populations it serves, in addition to increased medical services. The data in Figure 2.6 are from a study on children with asthma, and all statistical differences are significant ($p < .05$).

These statistics tell a story of how SCHIP can holistically help children and their families. The ability to see a doctor closer to home alleviates stress the family may feel in not having extra time to go to the doctor. Obtaining such an appointment is also easier because they are not forced to use an already overburdened community clinic. Since it is both easier to get to the doctor and easier to get an appointment, preventive medical treatment is more accessible. As such, any medication prescribed to prevent or cure illness is now easier to reach. Finally, since all are now fully supported and serving the people, poor health conditions would not be left to linger, thus requiring fewer visits to the emergency room (Szilagyi et al., 2006).

TABLE 2.8 Prior to SCHIP Implementation, Racial Differences in Health Care (Shone et al., 2005)				
	White	*Black*	*Hispanic*	*p value*
Has a primary source of care	94.8%	85.9%	80.5%	.000
Kept all/most appointments with primary source of care	61.2%	53.9%	33.9%	.001
Kept some/none of the appointments with primary source of care	38.8%	46.1%	66.1%	.001

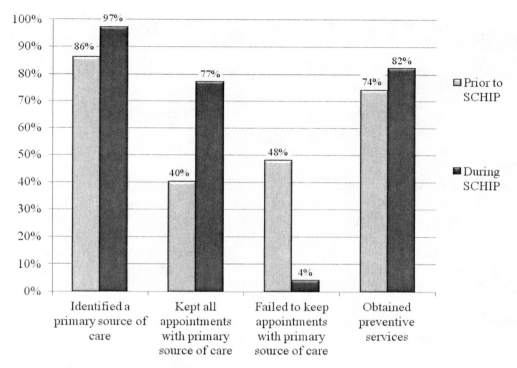

Figure 2.5   Health-Care Access, Before and After SCHIP

(Szilagyi, Dick, Klein, Shone, Zwanziger, & McInerny, 2004)

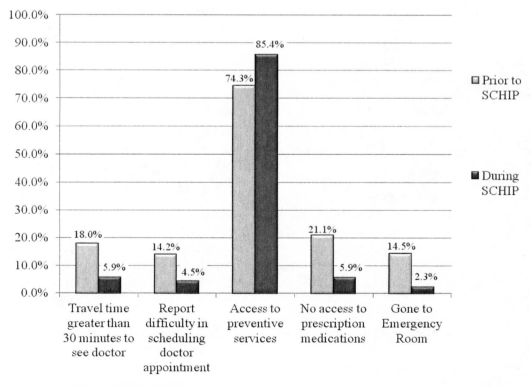

Figure 2.6   Before and After SCHIP, Other Benefits

(Szilagyi, Dick, Klein, Shone, Zwanziger, Bajorska, & Yoos, 2006)

TABLE 2.9
SCHIP and the Shrinking Racial Gaps in Health Care (Szilagyi et al., 2004)

	Has a Primary Source of Care		*Reports an Unmet Need*		*Obtained Preventive Services*	
	Before SCHIP	*After SCHIP*	*Before SCHIP*	*After SCHIP*	*Before SCHIP*	*After SCHIP*
White	92.6%	97.3%	25.2%	14.7%	67.1%	77.7%
Black	85.9%	94.9%	40.1%	17.0%	76.0%	86.5%
Hispanic	83.5%	98.3%	34.4%	19.3%	75.0%	79.0%

Moving from the general numbers that represent how SCHIP has broadly helped children gain access to medical care, the data in Table 2.9 detail the shrinking racial gap in health-care access thanks to the same program.

Table 2.9 is complicated and must be dissected at three levels. First, SCHIP helps each racial community. Every before-SCHIP/after-SCHIP difference is statistically significant, except for the White and Hispanic differences in the final field of "Obtained Preventive Services." For example, before SCHIP, 40.1% of Black children had an unmet health-care need; that number dove to 17% with SCHIP. The number of Hispanic children who had a primary source of care soared from only 83.5% before SCHIP to 98.3% after SCHIP. Each statistic is proof positive that SCHIP is needed and works (Szilagyi et al., 2004).

A second outcome of note is derived from Table 2.9. These numbers illustrate that when a social program aids a disenfranchised population, an often-occurring side benefit is that the social program also helps the dominant population. Before SCHIP, a quarter of White children had an unmet health-care need, with SCHIP it dropped to 14.7%. Additionally, only 67.1% of White children accessed preventive medicine before SCHIP, but following implementation of this program, that number rose to 77.7%. Many argue against social programs from the vantage point that a gain for one group comes at a cost for another. This is not true. SCHIP serves as the perfect example that a social program that assists children of color can also greatly benefit White children (Szilagyi et al., 2004).

The final takeaway from this complicated data set is that while SCHIP has drastically reduced the racial disparity gap in health-care access, it has not erased it. A gap still exists (Szilagyi et al., 2004). Plus, the aforementioned increase in medical participation assumes that when children of color increase their access to health care through SCHIP, this increase represents quality health care. Unfortunately, this is not always the case. As detailed in Figure 2.7, when patients rate the quality of their primary source of care, a statistically significant racial disparity reemerges.

These disparities are just as important as the disparities in access prior to SCHIP. Being able to go to a doctor is not enough; health care requires trust and investment of time. Especially for the Hispanic population, there are concerns about the patient being heard, receiving detailed medical explanations, feeling respected, and spending adequate time with a doctor. Perhaps language and cultural barriers account for these discrepancies (Shone et al., 2005), but the duty of care is carried by health-care professionals, and it is their responsibility to overcome these hurdles.

At every level, health insurance, Medicaid, and SCHIP have been unable to provide quality health care to all children. Some children remain uncovered by these programs and still others who are eligible are not enrolled (Kenney & Haley, 2001). Therefore it is still essential to rethink normative practices in disseminating health-care resources.

Persistent racial disparity has pushed health-care advocates away from a one-size-fits-all approach, toward individually tailored, community-focused endeavors. Some research points to the use of the Internet to disseminate medical information to underserved populations (Fulcher & Kaukinen, 2004). However, such endeavors are affected by the ever-increasing digital divide. Various communities, including those living in poverty and people of color, have inadequate access to computers (Brodie et al., 2000). For example, examining those living in urban metropolises, the U.S. Department of Commerce (2000) reported that Whites have much higher access to the Internet than do Blacks and Hispanics, as detailed in Figure 2.8.

Therefore, we cannot use technology and the Internet to solve this chronic and pervasive problem.

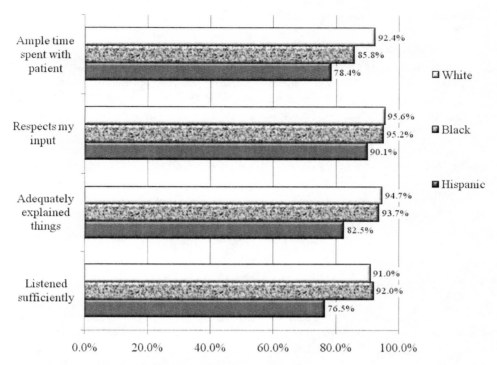

Figure 2.7 Patient Ratings of Primary Source of Care

(Shone et al., 2005)

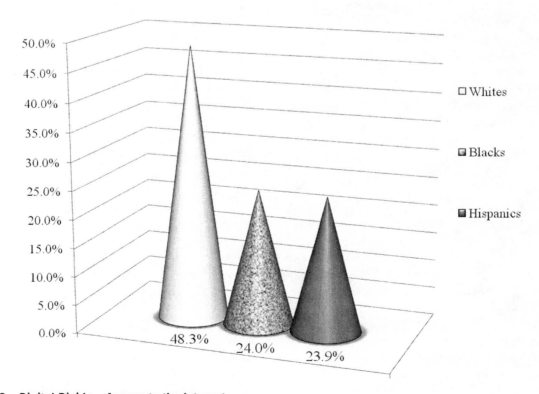

Figure 2.8 Digital Divide—Access to the Internet

(U.S. Department of Commerce, 2000)

Instead, we need direct human interaction to cure this uniquely created human problem. With this in mind, many professionals advocate a drastic makeover for pediatric medicine. We cannot assume any longer that opening a doctor's office in a historically underserved community will solve all of our problems. Even if it is built, patients still may not come.

David Satcher, Jeffrey Kaczorowski, and David Topa (2005) argue that if the "social, community, and environmental factors" that heavily influence a child's healthy living remain misunderstood, there will be a severe negative effect on a "pediatrician's ability to promote health and diagnose or treat disease adequately" (p. 1124). In such a dynamic, it is the poor children of color who stand to suffer disparate negative consequences. This is why it is of growing importance that pediatricians be proactive advocates for children.

The *Healthy People 2010* program brings together resources from federal and state governments as well as various not-for-profit organizations to serve disenfranchised populations. By setting specific goals aimed at disseminating information widely, and promoting health along with preventing disease, it hopes to take measured steps in eradicating racism and other discriminatory practices in medicine. Pediatricians are vital to this process; they must be out in the community, not merely to tell the masses what to do, but rather, to listen to what the community needs. Some communities lack sex education, others need help fighting obesity, and still others require mental health services (Satcher et al., 2005). Due to the diversity of our nation, it is imperative to take a Freirean approach and first learn from the people you wish to serve, before assuming you have something to teach them (Freire, 1970).

One group that takes this Freirean approach is the Accessible and Culturally Competent Health Care Project (ACCHCP). This organization sought to serve the rural Hispanic population in Walhalla, South Carolina. Such rural areas in South Carolina have some of the worst access to health services and, therefore, possess horrific health indicators:

- 20% more likely than urban residents to die of cancer;
- 50% more likely to die from prostate cancer than are urban residents; and
- 37% more likely than urban residents to die from heart problems (Sherrill et al., p. 3).

These largely adult medical issues also trickle down to affect children, with a 26% higher likelihood for rural citizens than for urban citizens to be admitted to a hospital for a preventable condition (Sherrill et al., 2005). In battling this reality, instead of relying on the traditional means of reaching the people, ACCHCP enlisted the people themselves to deliver their message. Employing the Promotora Model, ACCHCP hired 10 respected members of the community who were fluent in both Spanish and English and gave them extensive training in health services. These Promotoras then served as "health connectors" between ACCHCP and the community (p. 5). As members of the community, they were trustworthy sources who could educate their friends and neighbors in countless unplanned interactions. Whether it was in line at the grocery store, dropping kids off at school, or attending religious services, these Promotoras were poised to offer guidance on a wide range of health topics (Sherrill et al., 2005).

These new measures complement Medicaid and SCHIP and are essential to improving the health of children across the United States. A childhood filled with illness and little to no access to health care can greatly affect adult life expectancy. As of 2006 in the United States, Whites still had a longer life expectancy than Blacks (CDC, 2009). This disparity has become smaller over the past few decades, but its ever-present existence highlights that there is more work to be done. In fact, some researchers contend that our "most health-disadvantaged groups have life expectancies that are similar to some poor developing countries" (Murray, Kulkarni, & Ezzati, 2005, p. 6).

The United States cannot risk becoming complacent when there are still millions of children who go without satisfactory health services. Every woman, man, and child has the right to adequate health care, but not everyone is receiving it. To better understand this plight, we need to move beyond a wide-scope understanding of the health-care system and its effects on children of color, to a more focused examination of the specific facets of this disparity.

NEONATAL DEVELOPMENT

Widely accepted international indicators of population health are infant mortality rates (children who die in their first year of life) and birth weight (the weight of children when they are born). Those born with lower birth weights are at increased risk for health difficulties and death. Throughout U.S. history, there has been rampant disparity in these rates between Black and White babies (Ford et al., 2005; Shi, Macinko, Starfield, Politzer, & Xu, 2005). As the data from the Children's Defense Fund (2008) display in Figure 2.9, the infant mortality and low birth weight rate for Blacks is much higher than for Whites.

One might assume the extensive medical advances in the United States would pay huge dividends in lowering the ratio between Black and White infant mortality rates over time. However, in looking at the decade-by-decade data in Table 2.10, the ratio has gone up every 10 years except for one time. From 2000 on, for every one White baby death, there have been 2.47 Black baby deaths.

It may be tempting to conclude that these medical indicators have a biological root. After all, since this issue is pervasive throughout all 50 states, a genetic predisposition to higher infant death and lower birth

TABLE 2.10	
Infant Mortality Rate, Black-White Ratio	
(Children's Defense Fund, 2008)	
	Black-White Infant Mortality Ratio
1950	1.64
1960	1.93
1970	1.83
1980	2.04
1990	2.37
2000	2.47

weight would seem a fair conclusion; however, such belief systems hide injustice. Infant mortality is a socially created condition. At every level, Black women have worse birth outcomes than White women. Despite increases in Medicaid and other social programs, and despite the increased class standing of Black women, infant mortality rates are growing further apart. If this were a medical phenomenon, we could

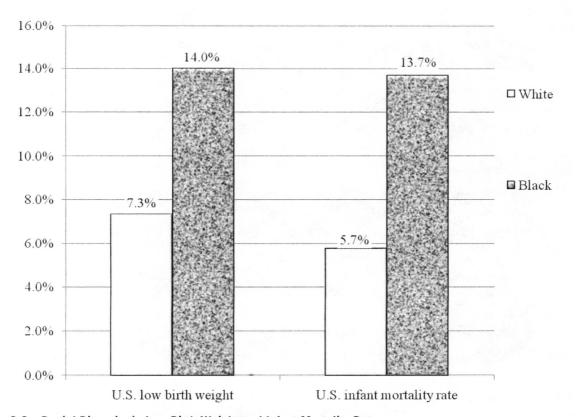

Figure 2.9   Racial Disparity in Low Birth Weight and Infant Mortality Rates

(Children's Defense Fund, 2008)

devote resources and research to find a solution and/ or cure. But, there is nothing to support that belief (Ford et al., 2005). Therefore, we need to understand the current complexity of this issue to improve future outcomes.

Most would argue that prenatal care should be an absolute right afforded to every pregnant mother. However, there is a statistically significant difference ($p < .05$) among people of color and Whites in this regard, and this directly affects the rates of premature birth and infant mortality (Masi, Hawkley, Piotrowski, & Pickett, 2007). These results are shown in Table 2.11.

Access to prenatal care is directly related to an individual's circumstances. As shown, expectant White mothers have a better chance of receiving prenatal care, thereby reducing the chance of delivering a premature baby and increasing the chance of a healthy birth weight. These numbers are statistically significant and indicate that racial disparity begins in the womb (Masi et al., 2007), even though they do not prove that the disparity is socially constructed. However, other research has done so.

If African Americans truly are biologically predisposed to worse birth outcomes, those numbers should also be reflected in Africans generally. One study, whose results are illustrated in Table 2.12, compared the difference in outcomes in twin births between African Americans and immigrants in the United States of African descent. At every level, the immigrant mothers of African descent had better outcomes, and the differences were statistically significant ($p < .0001$) (Salihu et al., 2005).

Parallel results were reported one year later, this time including Whites. Yet again, even with the cultural and language barriers present for immigrants of African descent, they still fare better than African Americans. A reason for this disparity could be that immigrants of African descent have not experienced the same negative effects of racism throughout their entire lives. However, the results in Table 2.13 also depict that while these immigrants fare better than African Americans, none are better off than Whites.

The source of this disparity cannot be found in the DNA of African Americans; the source is in the DNA

TABLE 2.11
Prenatal Care and Its Effects, Racial Disparity (Masi et al., 2007)

	White	Black	Hispanic
Prenatal care absent or administered in 3rd trimester	20.0%	37.0%	35.0%
Premature infant	6.3%	14.0%	7.2%
Infant weight at birth	3,402 grams	3,089 grams	3,342 grams

TABLE 2.12
Low Birth Weight and Preterm Birth, African American and Immigrants of African Descent (Salihu et al., 2005)

	African American	Immigrant of African Descent
Low birth weight	64.6%	54.0%
Preterm birth	57.9%	52.1%

TABLE 2.13
Effects of Access to Prenatal Care (Kramer, Ananth, Platt, & Joseph, 2006)

	White	African American	Immigrant of African Descent
Absent or late prenatal care	14.4%	23.7%	22.9%
Preterm birth of less than 37 weeks	9.3%	16.6%	12.6%
Infant birth mortality (per 1,000 children)	2.4	4.7	3.6

of this country. The inequality in neonatal development was not created at conception; it began long before. Many researchers have adopted a life-course perspective to explain this.

> The life-course perspective reconceptualizes determinants of birth outcomes longitudinally as part of the developmental process for reproductive health; it provides a longitudinal account of the interplay of biological, behavioral, psychological, and social protective and risk factors in producing adverse birth outcomes. (Lu & Halfon, 2003, p. 19)

In other words, the racist system that limits people of color's access to neonatal services is only one part of a growing snowball tumbling downhill. In understanding the pervasiveness of this problem, our next step is to examine access to preventive medicine.

PREVENTIVE MEDICINE

The National Survey on Early Childhood Health (NSECH) was conducted through the CDC (2008) to garner data "on the delivery of pediatric care to families with children under 3 years of age and the promotion of young children's health by families in their homes." Much of the data collected pertains to preventive medicine and healthy lifestyles for children and, as we've found in other studies, children of color were significantly less likely to benefit from such care.

There are two measures of interest from the NSECH. The first is Anticipatory Guidance and Parental Education (AGPE). This measure includes knowledge transfer in areas including:

- breastfeeding;
- how child communicates his or her needs;
- taking child off the bottle;
- bedtime routines;

- importance of reading to child; and
- immunizations (Bethell, Peck Reuland, Halfon, & Schor, 2004, p. 1982).

The second measure under review is Family-Centered Care (FCC). This measure encapsulates topics such as:

- Pediatric clinician takes time to understand the specific needs of child.
- Pediatric clinician respects the parent as an expert about his or her child.
- Pediatric clinician asks the parent how he or she is feeling as a parent.
- Pediatric clinician understands the parent and the child's family and how they prefer to raise the child (Bethell et al., 2004, p. 1983).

The topics in each of these measures are crucial to children's health and the confidence parents have in their medical providers. Table 2.14 shows that people of color report lower percentages of knowledge transferred via the AGPE measure and lower percentages of care and concern from pediatricians as indicated in the FCC measure.

I would contend that in both measures these numbers are too low for all children. However, given that there still is a statistically significant difference between these populations, children of color are perennially lower than Whites.

One aspect included in the NSECH that is the subject of a great amount of additional research is immunization. Luckily, the gap between White children and children of color has narrowed in the past decade, but has not closed entirely. Immunizations require repeated trips to the doctor's office, along with the money to pay for them. The typical childhood immunization series is called the 4:3:1:3:3, which stands for ">4 doses of diphtheria, tetanus toxoids, and pertussis vaccine, or diphtheria and tetanus toxoids; >3 doses of poliovirus vaccine; >1 dose of measles-containing vaccine; >3 doses of *Haemophilus influenzae* type b vaccine; and >3 doses of hepatitis B vaccine" (Darling,

TABLE 2.14 Racial Differences on AGPE and FCC Measures (Bethell et al., 2004)			
	White	*Hispanic*	*Black*
Anticipatory Guidance and Parental Education (AGPE)	50.2%	31.5%	38.8%
Family-Centered Care (FCC)	62.3%	49.8%	60.1%

Barker, Shefer, & Chu, 2005, p. 421–422). A CDC assessment called the National Immunization Study measures this 4:3:1:3:3 immunization coverage. The data in Figure 2.10 represent just three years and show the disparity closing, but not eliminated.

In this sampling of three years, we see closure in the immunization gap for Hispanics and Asians, with Black children still lagging more than 8% behind White children; this disparity illustrates the need for substantive change (Chu, Barker, & Smith, 2004).

Research has paid particular attention to the Hispanic population because of its rapid growth. In 2003 Hispanics accounted for 25% of all children born in the United States. However, their health coverage does not follow the same rate, as illustrated by a study on their access to the 4:3:1:3:3 immunization series. From 1996 through 2003, in every single year, except 2001, Hispanic children "were significantly less well immunized" than Whites (Darling et al., 2005, p. 423).

Furthermore, an interesting trend is represented within these statistics. Although it is true that across the United States there is a statistically significant difference between Hispanic and White children for inoculations, there are places in the country where more Hispanics are actually immunized than are Whites. In such instances there is a dual-layered explanation for this phenomenon. First, these communities, such as El Paso County in Texas, have a greater presence of community-based social programs. Second, this increase of community involvement appears to have an inverse relationship with the surrounding Hispanic population's degree of acculturation. This second factor brings forth an exceedingly interesting American dilemma: to acculturate/assimilate or not (Darling et al., 2005)?

The prescribed recipe for success in American immigration has long been acculturation. The message given to immigrants is that, if they melt into traditional American culture (aka White), they will advance their

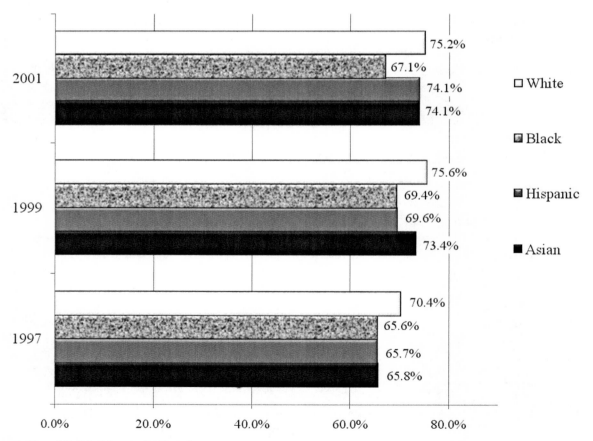

Figure 2.10   4:3:1:3:3 Immunization Coverage

(Chu, Barker, & Smith, 2004)

life station. And yet, for immunization, degree of acculturation was a negative correlation. Those communities with the highest degree of acculturation had the lowest immunization and, conversely, those with the lowest degree of acculturation had much higher immunization coverage. Such results are not new (Prislin, Suarez, Simpson, & Dyer, 1998) and run counter to the normative American Dream story. Advancement in the United States does not have to flow from a melting pot. A community united by a historically shared culture is more likely to design its own social services and show care and concern for its community members, which, in turn, increases the health of everyone (Darling et al., 2005).

Results like this remind us that while children of color may share many similar negative outcomes from society, they all have different stories. The umbrella term children of color gives us power to draw specific correlations and causalities, but it diminishes the group's diversity. Therefore, it is important to examine groups like Hispanics more closely to ascertain any intragroup differences.

Researchers have done this work in evaluating differential 4:3:1:3:3 inoculation rates for six different Hispanic groups. In Table 2.15, each specific inoculation rate in this series is broken down individually, showing wide differences among these groups (Herrera, Zhao, & Klevins, 2001).

This rich data set raises a host of concerns. Given that there can be as much as a 10% point gap within this group, any program designed to reach the Hispanic population must be individually tailored to different subgroups. This kind of research is also required for other groups, including, Blacks, Native Americans, and Asians, to discover the intragroup differences and community needs of these populations.

CONCLUSION

It is remarkable how resilient children can be. This is evident in the way they play. They will run, jump, skip, hop, and sometimes come crashing down to the floor with a velocity that would shatter my bones into a thousand pieces. Then children will jump up off the floor, racing in new directions like nothing happened. It is amazing every time.

Children are resilient, yes, but not indestructible. We cannot expect positive outcomes for children when they lack health insurance, do not see doctors, cannot obtain medications, and do not have access to inoculations. In addition to the health problems mentioned in this chapter, many more are running rampant throughout the United States (e.g., nutrition, mental health). The sum total of these negative life circumstances will dramatically affect a child's long-term development. Every child, regardless of the color of his or her skin, deserves quality health care, and statistics clearly illustrate that all children are not being treated equally in this regard.

REFERENCES

Bethell, C., Peck Reuland, C. H., Halfon, N., & Schor, E. L. (2004). Measuring the quality of preventative and developmental services for young children: National estimates and patterns of clinicians' performance. *Pediatrics, 113*(6), 1973–1983.

Brodie, M., Flournoy, R. E., Altman, D. E., Blendon, R. J., Benson, J. M., & Rosenbaum, M. D. (2000). Health information, the internet, and the digital divide. *Health Affairs, 19*(6), 255–265.

Centers for Disease Control and Prevention (CDC). (2008). *National Survey on Early Childhood Health.*

TABLE 2.15
Inoculation Differences Among Hispanic Population (Herrera et al., 2001)

	≥4 DTP	≥3 Poliovirus	≥1 Measles	≥3 Haemophilus influenzae type b	≥3 Hepatitis B
Mexican	77.6%	89.3%	89.0%	90.1%	82.4%
Puerto Rican	79.5%	89.7%	91.5%	92.1%	86.7%
Central American	72.7%	84.8%	86.5%	87.1%	79.8%
Cuban	78.6%	90.6%	87.3%	89.9%	84.6%
South American	85.3%	93.9%	96.3%	94.2%	90.5%
Dominican	87.3%	93.0%	96.8%	92.5%	89.3%

Next Steps for the Reader

- If you have health insurance, review your insurance claims for a six-month period and determine the health-care cost without insurance. If this amount of money is significant, determine what you would have gone without if forced to choose.
- Learn about the Affordable Care Act and how it affects not only children, but also yourself. This is the comprehensive health-care reform passed by Congress and signed into law by President Obama in March 2010.

Additional Resources for Up-to-Date Facts and Stats

Centers for Disease Control and Prevention
- Homepage—http://www.cdc.gov/
- National Center for Health Statistics—http://www.cdc.gov/nchs/
- National Immunization Survey—http://www.cdc.gov/nchs/nis.htm
- National Survey of Children's Health—http://www.cdc.gov/nchs/slaits/nsch.htm

Children's Defense Fund
- Homepage—http://www.childrensdefense.org/
- Black Community Crusade for Children—http://www.childrensdefense.org/programs-campaigns/black-community-crusade-for-children-II/

National Institutes of Health
- Homepage—http://health.nih.gov/
- PubMed: U.S. National Library of Medicine—http://www.ncbi.nlm.nih.gov/sites/entrez

U.S. Census Bureau
- Health Insurance—http://www.census.gov/hhes/www/hlthins/hlthins.html
- Health & Nutrition: Health Conditions, Diseases: http://www.census.gov/compendia/statab/cats/health_nutrition/health_conditions_diseases.html

U.S. Department of Health and Human Services
- Children's Health Insurance Program (CHIP)—http://www.cms.gov/home/chip.asp

World Health Organization
- Homepage—http://www.who.int/
- Child Health—http://www.who.int/topics/child_health/en/
- WHO Global Infobase—https://apps.who.int/infobase/

Retrieved from http://www.cdc.gov/nchs/slaits/nsech.htm

Centers for Disease Control and Prevention (CDC). (2009). *Health, United States, 2008: With special feature on the health of young adults.* Retrieved from http://www.cdc.gov/nchs/data/hus/hus08.pdf#026

Children's Defense Fund. (2008). *State of America's children 2008 report.* Retrieved from http://www.childrensdefense.org/child-research-data-publications/data/state-of-americas-children-2008-report-child-health-coverage.pdf

Chu, S. Y., Barker, L. E., & Smith, P. J. (2004). Racial/ethnic disparities in preschool immunizations: United States, 1996–2001. *American Journal of Public Health, 94*(6), 973–977.

Daniels, N. (2001). Justice, health, and healthcare. *The American Journal of Bioethics, 1*(2), 2–16.

Darling, N. J., Barker, L. E., Shefer, A. M., & Chu, S. Y. (2005). Immunization coverage among Hispanic ancestry, 2003 National Immunization Survey. *American Journal of Preventive Medicine, 29*(5), 421–427.

Drukker, M., Buka, S. L., Kaplan, C., McKenzie, K., & Van Os, J. (2005). Social capital and young adolescents' perceived health in different sociocultural settings. *Social Science & Medicine, 61*(1), 185–198.

Ford, B. C., Dalton, V. K., Lantz, P. M., Lori, J., Noll, T. O., Rodseth, S. B., . . . & Siefert, K. (2005). Racial disparities in birth outcomes: Poverty, discrimination, and the life course of African American women. *African American Research Perspectives, 10*(1), 1–11. Retrieved from http://www.rcgd.isr .umich.edu/prba/perspectives/fall2005/ford.pdf

Freire, P. (1970). *Pedagogy of the oppressed.* New York: Continuum International.

Fulcher, C. L., & Kaukinen, C. E. (2004). Visualizing the infrastructure of US healthcare using internet GIS: A community health informatics approach for reducing health disparities. *Studies in Health Technology and Informatics, 107*(2), 1197–1201.

Herrera, G. A., Zhao, Z., & Klevens, R. M. (2001). Variation in vaccination coverage among children of Hispanic ancestry. *American Journal of Preventative Medicine, 20*(4), 69–74.

Jablonski, K. A., & Guagliardo, M. F. (2005). Pediatric appendicitis rupture rate: A national indicator of disparities in healthcare access. *Population Health Metrics, 3*(4). Retrieved from http://www.pophealthmetrics .com/content/3/1/4

Kempe, A., Beaty, B. L., Crane, L. A., Stokstad, J., Barrow, J., Belman, S., & Steiner, J. F. (2005). Changes in access, utilization, and quality of care after enrollment into a state child health insurance plan. *Pediatrics, 115*(2), 364–371.

Kenney, G., & Haley, J. (2001). Why aren't more uninsured children enrolled in Medicaid or SCHIP? *The Urban Institute,* Series B (B-35), 1–7.

Kramer, M. S., Ananth, C. V., Platt, R. W,. & Joseph, K. S. (2006). US Black vs White disparities in fetal growth: Physiological or pathological? *International Journal of Epidemiology, 35*(5), 1187–1195.

Lu, M. C., & Halfon, N. (2003). Racial and ethnic disparities in birth outcomes: A life-course perspective. *Maternal and Child Health Journal, 7*(1), 13–30.

Martinez, M. E., & Cohen, R. A. (2008). *Health insurance coverage: Early release of estimates from the National Health Interview Survey, January–June 2008.* Centers for Disease Control and Prevention, National Center for Health Statistics. Retrieved from http://www.cdc.gov/nchs/data/nhis/earlyrelease/insur 200903.pdf

Masi, C. M., Hawkley, L. C., Piotrowski, Z. H., & Pickett, K. E. (2007). Neighborhood economic disadvantage, violent crime, group density, and pregnancy out-

comes in a diverse, urban population. *Social Science & Medicine, 65*(12), 2440–2457.

Murray, C. J., Kulkarni, S., & Ezzati, M. (2005). Eight Americas: New perspectives on U.S. health disparities. *American Journal of Preventive Medicine, 29*(5S1), 4–10.

Newacheck, P. W., Hughes, D. C., Hung, Y. Y., Wong, S., & Stoddard, J. J. (2000). The unmet health needs of America's children. *Pediatrics, 105*(4), 989–997.

Newacheck, P. W., McManus, M., Fox, H. B., Hung, Y. Y., & Halfon, N. (2000). Access to health care for children with special health care needs. *Pediatrics, 105*(4), 760–766.

Obama, B. (2009, February 4). *Remarks by President Barack Obama on Children's Health Insurance Program bill signing.* Presented at the White House, Washington D.C. Retrieved from http://www.whitehouse.gov/ the_press_office/RemarksbyPresidentBarackObama OnChildrensHealthInsuranceProgramBillSigning/

Prislin, R., Suarez, L., Simpson, D. M., & Dyer, J. A. (1998). When acculturation hurts: The case of immunization. *Social Science & Medicine, 47*(12), 1947–1956.

Salihu, H. M., Mardenbrough-Gumbs, W. S., Aliyu, M. H., Sedjro, J. E., Pierre-Louis, B. J., Kirby, R. S., & Alexander, G. R. (2005). Influence of nativity on neonatal survival on Black twins in the United States. *Ethnicity & Disease, 15*(2), 276–282.

Satcher, D., Kaczorowski, J., & Topa, D. (2005). The expanding role of the pediatrician in improving child health in the 21st century. *Pediatrics, 115*(4), 1124–1128.

Sherrill, W., Crew, L., Mayo, R. M., Rogers, B. L. & Haynes, D. F. (2005). Educational and health services innovation to improve care for rural Hispanic communities in the USA. *The International Electronic Journal of Rural and Remote Health Research, Education, Practice and Policy,* 5, 1–11.

Shi, L., Macinko, J., Starfield, B., Politzer, R., & Xu, J. (2005). Primary care, race, and mortality in US states. *Social Science & Medicine, 61*(1), 65–75.

Shone, L. P., Dick, A. W., Klein, J. D., Zwanziger, J., & Szilagyi, P. G. (2005). Reduction in racial and ethnic disparities after enrollment in the State Children's Health Insurance Program. *Pediatrics, 115*(6), 697–705.

Stout, D. (2007). Bush vetoes children's health bill. *New York Times.* Retrieved from http://www.nytimes.com/ 2007/10/03/washington/03cnd-veto.html

Strickland, B., McPherson, M., Weissman, G., van Dyck, P. Huang, Z. J., & Newacheck, P. (2004). Access to medical home: Results of the National Survey of

Children with Special Healthcare Needs. *Pediatrics,* *113*(5), 1485–1492.

Szilagyi, P. G., Dick, A. W., Klein, J. D., Shone, L. P., Zwanziger, J., Bajorska, A., & Yoos, H. L. (2006). Improved asthma care after enrollment in the State Children's Health Insurance Program in New York. *Pediatrics, 117*(2), 486–496.

Szilagyi, P. G., Dick, A. W., Klein, J. D., Shone, L. P., Zwanziger, J., & McInerny, T. (2004). Improved access and quality of care after enrollment in the New York State Children's Health Insurance Program (SCHIP). *Pediatrics, 113*(5), 395–404.

U.S. Department of Commerce. (2000). *Falling through the net: Toward digital inclusion.* Retrieved from http://www.ntia.doc.gov/ntiahome/fttn00/Falling.htm#2.1

U.S. Department of Health & Human Services. (2006). *Medicaid Program—General Information.* Retrieved from http://www.cms.hhs.gov/MedicaidGenInfo/01_Overview.asp#TopOfPage

U.S. Department of Health & Human Services. (2009). *The Children's Health Insurance Program (CHIP).* Retrieved from http://www.cms.hhs.gov/LowCost HealthInsFamChild/

Weinick, R. M., & Krauss, N. A. (2000). Racial/ethnic differences in children's access to care. *American Journal of Public Health, 90*(11), 1771–1774.

Welna, D. (2007). Bush vetoes child health care bill. *National Public Radio.* Retrieved from http://www.npr.org/templates/story/story.php?storyId=14938419

3

Race, Space, and Place
Environmental Justice

SOCIETY MAKES COUNTLESS DECISIONS ABOUT CHILdren's health even before they are conceived. Across the United States, families live amid air and water pollution, waste disposal sites, airports, smokestacks, lead paint, car emissions, and countless other environmental hazards (Lee, 2002; United Church of Christ Commission for Racial Justice, 1987). However, exposure to these toxins is not shared equally among our population. Studies show that these environmental conditions disproportionately affect people of color and the poor. Such inequity is at the core of the movement for environmental justice (Bullard, 1990).

Environmental justice is a field that has grown tremendously over the past two decades. While several different definitions exist, for the purposes of this chapter, environmental justice will combine two distinct facets. First, environmental justice is the movement investigating the disproportionate likelihood that people of color and those of lower SES will unduly bear exposure to negative environmental conditions (Bowen & Wells, 2002; Bullard, 1990; Masterton-Allen & Brown, 1990). Second, these conditions are part of a larger social system in which communities with lower social status experience discrimination and disenfranchisement (Capek, 1993; Pulido, 2000).

Many credit the United Church of Christ for taking the first definitive step in forming the environmental justice movement. In 1987 this organization published *Toxic Wastes and Race in the United States*, and then a follow-up report 20 years later, *Toxic Wastes and Race at 20: 1987–2007* (Bullard, Mohai, Saha, & Wright, 2007). Both reports detail realities such as the proximity of landfills and toxic waste sites to communities of color and the linked negative health consequences. This foundational work institutionalized the term environmental racism, which is now more commonly called environmental justice.

With this movement building momentum, the First National People of Color Environment Leadership summit was held in 1991. This summit created a document, entitled *The Principles of Environmental Justice* whose 17 principles clearly outlined the expectations the summit had for achieving environmental justice. They included the strict enforcement of laws and policies to be free from racism, the right for all people to determine the parameters of their own lives, and the right to remuneration when injured (People of Color Environmental Leadership Summit, 1991).

As hoped, the work of these organizations affected governing bodies. First, the United Nations (1992) published the *Rio Declaration on Environment and Development*, outlining 27 principles, including peoples' right not to be exploited in the name of development, peoples' right to access information regarding the environment, and adequate compensation to all victims of environmental hazards (Cutter, 1995). Then, in 1994, following this declaration from the international community, President Clinton signed Executive Order 12898, *Federal Actions to Address Environmental Justice in Minority Populations and Low-Income Populations.*

President Clinton also signed Executive Order 13045 in 1997, *Protection of Children From Environmental Health Risks and Safety Risks*, acknowledging the special status of children in this struggle.

These initiatives prompted a great deal of scientific and sociologic research. While data sets are complicated and at times conflict with one another, the breadth of research exemplifies the disparate experiences of people of color and low-SES populations when compared to the dominant population.

Some of the research attempts to separate people of color from low-SES communities, asserting that one group is more affected than the other: this chapter refutes this division for two reasons. First, it is often advantageous to the dominant hierarchy to have subsets of the disenfranchised at odds with one another. This is the classic divide-and-conquer strategy. However, these two groups are not in competition; they are both victims. As outlined by Liam Downey (1998), differential results between race and class are often functions of decisions in research methodology, such as where the research was conducted or how participants were solicited.

Second, I do not exclude either race or class from discussions of environmental justice because of their high covariance. Whether it is disease, death, access to health care, prenatal care, immunization, or other related lifestyle circumstances, "it is often difficult to distinguish the separate effects of class and race" (Sexton & Adgate, 1999, p. 4). Thus, dividing those victimized by environmental injustice is counterproductive.

In addition to conducting research, those advocating for environmental justice have created four specific rights for disenfranchised populations. These populations have the right to:

1. accurate information about the situation;
2. a prompt, respectful, and unbiased hearing when contamination claims are made;
3. democratic participation in deciding the future of the contaminated community; and
4. compensation from parties who have inflicted injuries on the victims (Capek, 1993, p. 8).

The assertion of these rights has been foundational in the environmental justice movement.

Clear scientific data support all the assertions of the environmental justice movement. I expect opponents of environmental justice to quickly point out that science cannot prove beyond all reasonable doubt that discriminatory environmental conditions are the cause of any health problems for disenfranchised populations. However, I would also highlight that absolute proof is a status science never reaches. Scientists cannot definitively prove that smoking causes cancer or that pollution is causing global warming; however, the objective of science is to look at broad research trends and make judicious assertions.

The data and maps offered in the following pages present several specific case studies of afflicted communities within the United States. Each map was created using OpenStreetMap and the Environmental Protection Agency's online EnviroMapper tool. OpenStreetMap serves as the background for each map, and the information inputted for entities such as hazardous waste sites and schools was provided by the EPA (n.d.). In concluding this chapter, we detail how these environmental conditions negatively affect children; the most notable outcome is asthma.

ENVIRONMENTAL JUSTICE CASE STUDIES

Ponca City, Oklahoma

Ponca City, Oklahoma, is home to two large companies that provide many jobs, along with a great deal of pollution, to this community. One of the businesses, Continental Carbon Company, creates a rubber compound known as carbon black. Depicted in Figure 3.1,

Figure 3.1   Carbon Black Powder

(FK1954, 2009)

carbon black is a miniscule black powder used in making tires and for coloring plastics and paper.

Although ownership of Continental Carbon Company has changed over the years, this factory has been producing carbon black at this location since the mid-1950s. A community of Native Americans on the Osage Indian Reservation is adjacent to this facil- ity, some with homes within 100 yards (Shriver & Webb, 2009). Figure 3.2 depicts this close proximity.

The powder from carbon black production paints everything around it black. Residents breathe and digest this substance throughout their lives. Although White families, who live farther from the facility, have won compensation for the negative health consequences

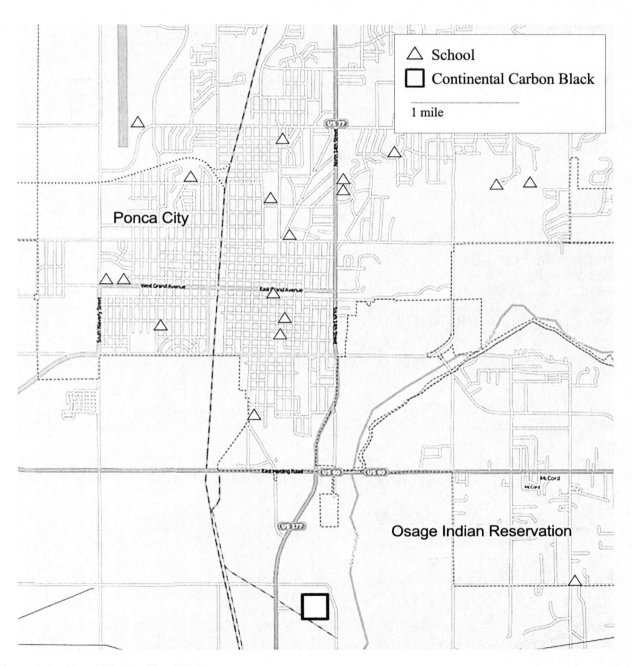

Figure 3.2 Map of Ponca City, Oklahoma

they've experienced from exposure to carbon black, the Native American community has been unsuccessful in this regard. It has been ignored by the legal system and the agency set up to be its advocate—Indian Health Services (Shriver & Webb, 2009). In addition, as in many similar cases throughout the United States, children bear the brunt. All of the 18 schools in the area are within five miles of this facility, as depicted in Figure 3.2, and children have no choice but to attend them.

For this community, trying to keep their homes clean is a constant chore. Some have forgone carpeting because of the impossible task of keeping it clean, opting instead to live right on the subflooring of their houses. When the children living in these homes walk through the house, their feet turn jet black. Their parents have been forced to use mechanic's soap to wash off the black soot. But it isn't the child's feet that are worrisome (Shriver & Webb, 2009). One mother of three shared:

> They've all had chronic problems. They all have runny noses, it's a constant. [Child's name] had ear infections all the time. [Child's name] had asthma and bronchitis all the time. [Child's name] [has] been in the hospital twice. He's been hospitalized for asthma, pneumonia, bronchitis, scarlet fever. He's four. (pp. 279–280)

Respiratory problems are so commonplace that the neighborhood children know how to give themselves breathing treatments. One of these children is only two years old (Shriver & Webb, 2009).

The damaging effects of breathing in this air pollution are well documented. One Boston, Massachusetts, study found when children have prolonged exposure to "ultrafine and fine particles" in air pollution, it has disastrous effects on development (Suglia, Gryparis, Wright, Schwartz, & Wright, 2008, p. 280). This contact with air pollution "was associated with decreases in cognitive test scores, even after adjustment for socioeconomic status, birth weight, tobacco smoke exposure, and blood lead level" (p. 283).

For the residents of Ponca City, the chronic and pervasive nature of the dust produced from carbon black has also hindered the psychosocial development of the community. Many parents are reticent to allow the children to play outside; some have developed strategies of checking the wind conditions. One mother stated, "Yeah, on Tuesday or Wednesday I kept the lit-

tle ones in because the wind was blowing straight over the facility back there. It was gross" (Shriver & Webb, 2009, p. 279). Other parents are less flexible, opting instead to keep their children inside at all times. This step severely limits the child's interactions with others, ultimately hindering optimal social development (Shriver & Webb, 2009).

Many parties have pulled together to raise the profile of this environmental injustice. Tribal leaders and politicians are involved in lobbying efforts, federal lawsuits have been filed, and one filmmaker created a documentary on the plight of this community, entitled *Black Sky, White Eagle* (Shriver & Webb, 2009). In advocating for his community, the Ponca Tribal Chairman emphatically stated:

> The Continental Carbon Company has exhibited a callous disregard towards the Ponca Tribe of Indians and our people by continuing to pollute our people, our lands, and our air. The Ponca Tribe was forced to take this land at gunpoint by the government, and now it is all we have left. (Norrell, 2005)

As of yet, this community goes unaided, while the health of its children keeps deteriorating.

Carver Terrace Neighborhood, Texarkana, Texas

Carver Terrace is a revealing example of a community that stood up to the government and successfully confronted environmental injustice. However, as will be seen, success does not necessarily ensure justice.

This small neighborhood of 33 acres had 78 homes and was home to an African American middle- and working-class community. Texarkana is split between Texas and Arkansas and is home to three Superfund sites (Figure 3.3), a landfill, and a nearby pollution-rich paper company. The federal government created the term Superfund to label the most heavily contaminated land that is particularly toxic and harmful to humans. In 1967, Carver Terrace was zoned as an area within Texarkana in which African Americans could buy homes. The first African Americans who moved in considered it a privilege to be able to buy their own home in an area "with amenities such as paved streets, playgrounds . . . and other desirable features at an affordable price" (Capek, 1993, p. 10).

In 1979, following a report to Congress on the hazardous waste from the nation's principal chemical com-

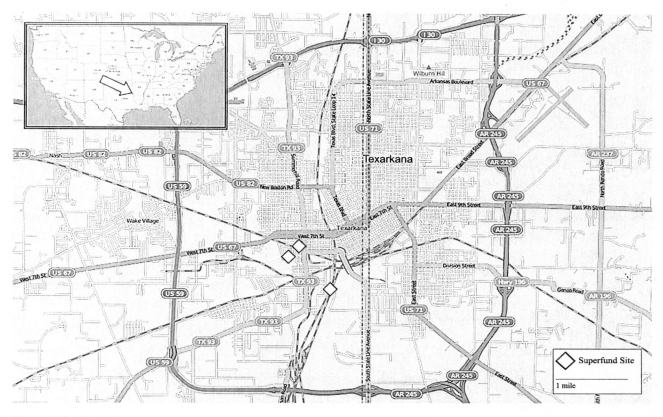

Figure 3.3   Texarkana

(EPA, n.d; © OpenStreetMap contributors, CC-BY-SA)

panies, the EPA became aware of an issue in Texarkana. Various toxins were found in the ground, but it was not until 1980 that the Department of Water Resources called for the area to be declared a Superfund. The EPA did not heed this Superfund recommendation for four more years. Despite the data and warnings, "many residents were unaware of the seriousness of the contamination until they read about it in the newspaper" (Capek, 1993, p. 11). It was not until 1991 that the Texas Department of Health began to study the potential health effects on the residents of this area. Researchers found that those living in Carver Terrace had a higher incidence of recurrent bronchitis, rash, liver disease, and premature and low birth weight babies (Capek, 1993).

As outlined earlier, the environmental justice movement has posited four rights that disenfranchised populations must possess. At each level, the residents of Carver Terrace had their rights violated. First, all people have the right to information; however, many residents received their information from newspapers and

neighbors. The EPA reported that, "the contamination posed no serious danger to residents" (Capek, 1993, p. 11). Second, all people have a right to a fair hearing. Residents had filed lawsuits against the corporations that contaminated the land; however, they soon learned how difficult it would be to take on a large corporation. In one lawsuit, a company brought in a doctor to testify that the health problems seen in Carver Terrace were a function of African American hereditary problems, not chemical contamination. At the end of that case, a White male juror reported he did not believe the Black man who filed the lawsuit "deserved that kind of money" (Capek, 1993, p. 14.) Third, all people can expect full democratic participation in plotting the future of the afflicted community. The residents of Carver Terrace achieved this right, but only through their own grassroots movements. Both informal social networks and formal organizations, like the Carver Terrace Community Action Group, advocated against the enveloping silence from the state and federal government, the EPA, and the involved corporations. The final right is compensation, something residents of Carver Terrace eventually did receive. A federal buyout ensued and the first residents moved out in 1992. Although many residents felt they did not receive fair market value for their home, all gained the opportunity to leave this community (Capek, 1993).

Some may term the eventual outcome of the Carver Terrace neighborhood a success. However, this so-called success cost some people their lives, lowered the quality of life for others, splintered a strong community, and exemplified the bureaucracy and time involved in government intervention (Capek, 1993).

Louisiana

A complete report on issues of environmental justice in Louisiana would include a full overview of the historical markers that have led to the creation of a Cancer Alley through this state. Slavery, plantations,

Jim Crow, segregation, and government corruption all have played their part in creating this plight. Even considering all of this, today's problems are shocking. Louisiana is poor. As Figure 3.4 shows, in 2004, the national poverty rate was 12.1%; Louisiana's was 17.5%, the fourth-highest in the entire country. A total of 26.4% of the children in Louisiana live in poverty, the second-highest in the nation (Wright, 2005).

Some have gone so far as to call the state of Louisiana a third world country (Roberts & Toffolon-Weiss, 2001). Adding to this plight, the state and federal governments' collusion with petrochemical and chemical industries has afflicted residents for years (Wright, 2005).

The Mississippi corridor through Louisiana produces 20% of the United States' petrochemicals. Plants sprang up all along the water since it was easy to get barges down the river and out to the ocean. This also enabled companies to dispose of waste right into the

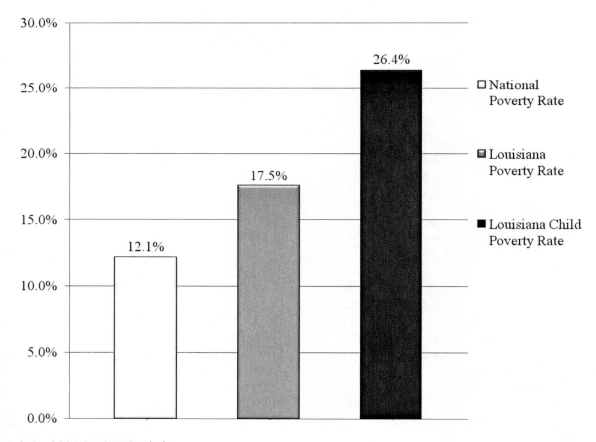

Figure 3.4 2004 Poverty Statistics

(Wright, 2005)

river. Everywhere in between these plants are schools, shopping malls, office buildings, parks, and people, setting up prime conditions for health deterioration (Wright, 2005).

There are too many examples of communities in which safety has been disregarded. In Taft, Louisiana, Hooker Chemical reportedly dumped asbestos and chlorine (Szaz, 1994). Alsen, Louisiana, is a predominantly African American community situated next to Rollins Hazardous Waste Treatment and Disposal Facility. People of the community were forced to wear gas masks to protect their lungs from harmful carcinogens when the wind blew across this facility. In fact, as depicted in Figure 3.5, there are just as many schools (two) as there are Superfund sites (two) within one mile of Rollins, exemplifying the toxic conditions surrounding children of color residing in that community.

For a final example, the 20 parishes at the end of the Mississippi River possess 2,000 deposits of oil waste, along with many other hazardous waste sites. Many of the poor and disenfranchised in this bayou fish to defray the costs of food, putting them at even greater risk for health complications (Roberts & Toffolon-Weiss, 2001). Figure 3.6 depicts the area where the Mississippi River runs between Baton Rouge and New Orleans. Among all of the creeks and tributaries that feed into the Mississippi, which then empties into the Gulf of Mexico, are dozens of Superfund sites.

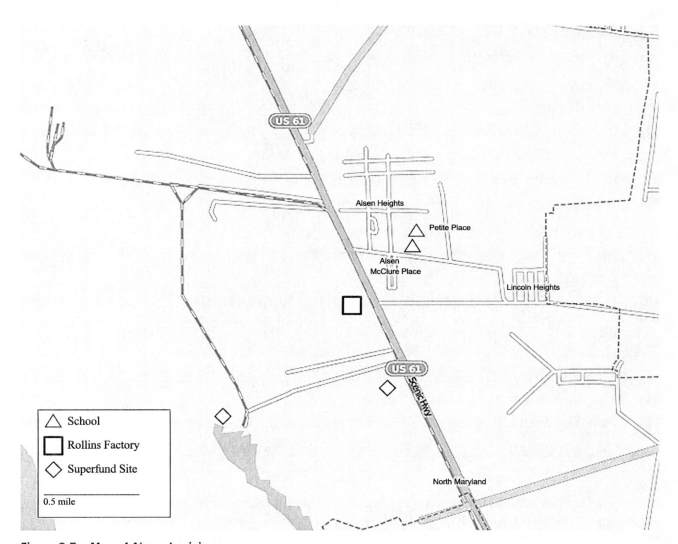

Figure 3.5   Map of Alsen, Louisiana

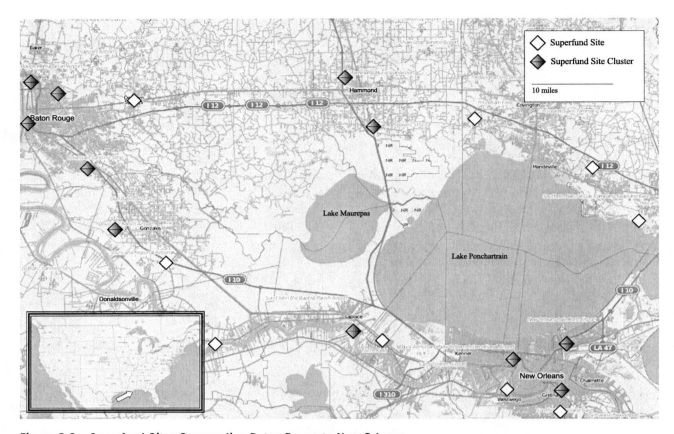

Figure 3.6   Superfund Sites Surrounding Baton Rouge to New Orleans

(EPA, n.d; © OpenStreetMap contributors, CC-BY-SA)

In recent decades, the state of Louisiana created organizations such as the Louisiana Department of Environmental Quality (LDEQ). However, as recently as 1997 the EPA stated that the agency did not adequately enforce regulations on everything from clean air to hazardous waste disposal (Roberts & Toffolon-Weiss, 2001).

Following Hurricane Katrina and the BP oil spill, all of these adverse environmental conditions have multiplied beyond all ability to calculate. Specifically, the dismal government response following Katrina is a lesson that can never be forgotten and created an environmental disaster that will never be undone.

Chicago, Illinois

As a native Chicagoan, I find it particularly painful to report that "Chicago and nearby suburbs face some of the highest risks . . . for cancer, lung disease and other health problems linked to toxic chemicals pouring from industry smokestacks" (Hawthorne & Little, 2008). The EPA has conducted extensive studies of my home city and concluded that it is one of the 10 worst in the nation. Even the collar counties rank in the 50 worst in the nation. And, shocking enough, the majority of the pollution emitted in and around Chicago is perfectly legal (Hawthorne & Little, 2008).

One afflicted community is Altgeld Gardens, a predominantly African American neighborhood on the South Side of the city. In the eight miles surrounding Altgeld are almost two dozen of the area's largest environmental polluters. One resident spoke: "We see and smell and live with this pollution every day. I may not have a science degree, but it isn't good" (Hawthorne & Little, 2008). Yet, the plight of Altgeld predates the current air pollution; the story begins with building this community on toxic land.

This housing project was built in 1945 on a landfill and at the edge of another sanitary dump. In truth, Altgeld is not all that different from other South Side areas sectioned off for people of color and the poor to live; many companies have used these neighborhoods as a dumpsite for nearly 140 years

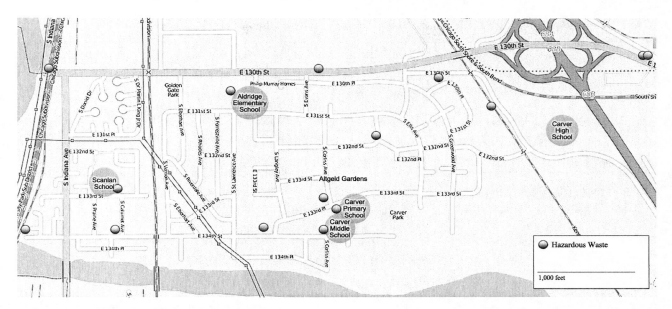

Figure 3.7   Altgeld Gardens, Chicago, Illinois

(EPA, n.d; © OpenStreetMap contributors, CC-BY-SA)

(Pellow, 2002). Figure 3.7 illustrates the hazardous waste sites situated in close proximity to schools in this neighborhood.

The land just west of Carver Park has three hazardous waste sites as labeled by the EPA and is where George Washington Carver Primary School currently sits. This school's students are 99.2% Black and 100% low-income (Chicago Public Schools, 2010). Figure 3.8 contains a picture of this educational institution.

Figure 3.8   Picture of George Washington Carver Primary School, Chicago, Illinois

(Stewart, 2011)

With such systemic environmental deterioration, the EPA has evaluated 42 South Side sites for classification as Superfunds, and 36 are governed by the Resource Conservation and Recovery Act of 1976 (Pellow, 2002). This Act instituted measures to address the clustering of cities and industrial waste sites and its deteriorating effect on health (Resource Conservation and Recovery Act, 1976).

The South Side of Chicago has inordinately high percentages of low birth weight births and high rates of infant mortality. When one mother was asked how long her son had been sick she stated, "Well, he was sick when he was born" (Pellow, 2002, p. 69). Additionally, for adults, one study concluded that the South Side of Chicago has a cancer rate nearly double that of the rest of the city (Pellow, 2002).

Just within Chicago city limits, there are 162 highly toxic areas identified, and 99 of them are neighborhoods comprised predominantly of people of color. Furthermore, 80% of garbage dumped illegally in Chicago occurs at the curbs and in the parks in people-of-color neighborhoods. Residents attempt to do their own cleanup, but picking up garbage will not fix the

damage already done to the soil. The same mother who remarked about her sick child stated, "You can't grow vegetables out here and you can't keep flowers out here. It don't grow" (Pellow, 2002, p. 69).

The Belmont Learning Complex

This final case study pertains to the construction of the Belmont Learning Complex, now called the Edward R. Roybal Learning Center, and specifically links an environmental injustice with the lives of children. This institution is pictured in Figure 3.9 and mapped in Figure 3.10.

In June 1997, construction began on this facility to help ease the overcapacity of schools in predominantly Latino neighborhoods of Los Angeles. In a far-reaching plan, developers planned to include a shopping mall and 120 apartment units to continue to support the community. At a projected cost of $200 million, the Belmont Learning Complex was called "the most expensive school in America" (Anderson, 2000, p. 32). It was revealed halfway through construction that the school site was a former oil field, one still active with "methane gas leaks and soil contamination with car-

Figure 3.9 Picture of Edward R. Roybal Learning Center, Los Angeles, California

(Ayrapetyan, 2010)

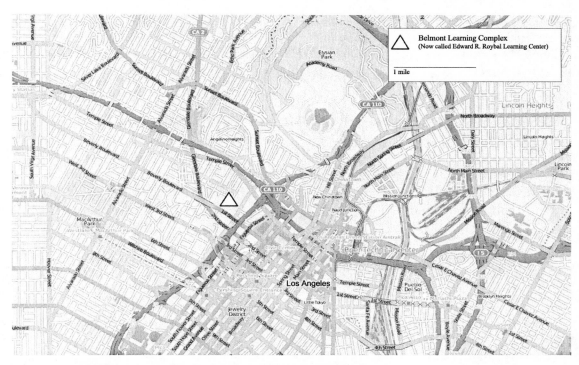

Figure 3.10   Map of Belmont Learning Complex, Los Angeles, California

(EPA, n.d; © OpenStreetMap contributors, CC-BY-SA)

cinogenic compounds" (Pastor, Sadd, & Morello-Frosch, 2002, p. 264). Children reported that, "fumes were so strong, we used to hold our noses and run home" (Anderson, 2000, p. 34). The developers knew about these environmental issues, but they chose to ignore the potential health effects of such toxins. After spending $123 million, the Board of Education shut down construction and fired the superintendent. Nonetheless, the community was still shocked at the disregard for the safety of its children. Unfortunately, this is not the only environmental justice issue in Los Angeles Unified School District (LAUSD) (Anderson, 2000; Pastor et al., 2002).

In a study of children's exposure to toxins in the greater LAUSD, Latino students were far more likely to go to a school near a high-capacity treatment storage and disposal facility (TSDF) and/or a Toxic Release Inventory (TRI) 33/50 facility. A high-capacity TSDF is a facility that processes more than 50 tons of hazardous materials per year. A TRI is a yearly record of the number of pounds of toxic chemicals emitted into the environment by a facility. The designation 33/50 denotes specific inclusion of 17 toxic chemicals the EPA is seeking to lower by half in environmental emission. The statistics in Table 3.1 describe this plight (Pastor et al., 2002, p. 271).

In both cases, the Latino population's overrepresentation was statistically significant ($p < .01$). These schools are making Latino children throughout Los Angeles susceptible to a lifetime of higher cancer risk,

TABLE 3.1 Schools and Proximity to a TSDF Site or TRI 33/50 Release Facility (Pastor et al., 2002)				
Percentage of School Population				
	White	*Black*	*Latino*	*Asian*
High-capacity TSDF within 1 mile of school	2.0%	8.4%	85.1%	4.1%
TRI 33/50 release facility within 1 mile of school	4.6%	12.5%	77.5%	4.6%

along with an increased likelihood of developing asthma. Furthermore, there is a link between respiratory problems, like asthma, and poor academic performance (Pastor et al., 2002).

THE EFFECT OF A TOXIC ENVIRONMENT ON CHILDREN

The story of the Belmont Learning Complex and associated issues throughout the LAUSD serve as a powerful starting point for discussing the specific health effects pollutants and toxins have on children. This hidden social plight is causing low birth weights along with premature births, hindering neurological development, severely debilitating children's respiratory health, and contributing to the development of cancer (Northwest Coalition for Alternatives to Pesticides, 2000). And statistics confirm that through every phase of their development, children of color suffer the worst effects of environmental injustice.

Prolonged exposure to toxins has immediate and long-term effects on children. From birth through the late teenage years, the brain and nervous system continue to develop, and both can be adversely affected by a toxic environment. However, the negative effects do not stop there. Organs such as the liver and kidneys cannot process toxins quickly, leaving them to linger and cause more harm. In addition, children's immune systems are still under development, making them more prone to sickness and infection. Last, children breathe at a faster rate than adults do, even when taking into account body size. Their higher need for oxygen increases the amounts of toxins taken into their lungs and filtered into the bloodstream. Affected children are more susceptible to immediate ailments such as "headaches, rashes, allergic reactions, asthma attacks, nausea, fevers, and other flu-like symptoms," along with longer-term consequences, including cancer and impairment of brain development (Northwest Coalition for Alternatives to Pesticides, 2000, p. 3).

One of every four children in the United States lives within a one-mile diameter of a hazardous waste site documented on the National Priority List, and Latino, Black, and Native American children are vastly overrepresented in this population. The National Environment Trust (2000) detailed this disproportionate amount of exposure to developmental toxins. This group identified the top 25 counties in the United

States that released such toxins; these counties possess 46% of all developmental toxic emissions for the whole country. In 14 of these counties, the Black population was disproportionately higher. Such exposure causes:

- a 6% increase in very low birth weight babies;
- a 4.6 % increase in premature babies;
- a doubling in the reporting of a specific heart defect—atrial septal defect;
- a 1.6 times increase in urinary tract blockages;
- an increase in diagnoses of attention deficit hyperactivity disorder (ADHD); and
- a doubling in the occurrences of Autism (National Environment Trust, 2000).

Many schools are located on some of the most poisoned landscapes in our country and have population densities greater than the majority of office buildings. This intensifies their effect upon children. As exemplified in the Belmont Learning Complex, schools are often built on toxic land; near TSDFs; and adjacent to airports, freeways, and garbage dumps. This type of land is low-cost, and cities, counties, and states often look for the cheapest land possible to build educational infrastructure. After constructing the school, pesticides are sprayed on the ground, walls, ceilings, and floors. The cheapest and harshest chemicals are used in cleaning, and, if there is an external playground, it is peppered with weed killer and fertilizer. Additionally, the buildings are typically equipped with low-grade ventilation systems that invite mold, adding to air pollution (Child Proofing Our Communities Campaign, 2001).

There are countless examples of how such conditions affect children. Mary McLeod Bethune Elementary School serves a predominantly Black community in Jacksonville, Florida. The school was built on a former incinerator-ash-dumping site that contaminated the ground. Figure 3.11 exemplifies how close this school is to a Superfund site.

The Sunnyside Unified School District in Tucson, Arizona, educates a largely Mexican American community. The industrial contamination of this area dates back so far that students from the 1950s had higher rates of cancer and leukemia. Then, in the early 1980s, the authorities shut down water wells used by this school district due to contamination from a toxin called trichloroethylene (TCE). Local military contrac-

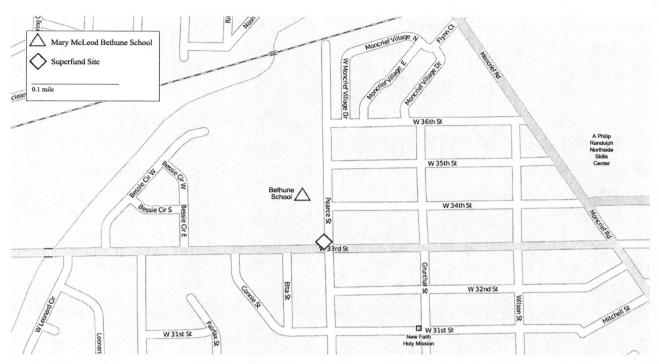

Figure 3.11   Mary McLeod Bethune Elementary School, Jacksonville, Florida

(EPA, n.d; © OpenStreetMap contributors, CC-BY-SA)

tors were responsible for this toxin seeping into the water supply. The current environmental concern stems from a business called Brush Ceramic Products, which has military contracts to process a metal called beryllium, a known cause of lung disease (see Figure 3.12). There are 25 schools within three miles of this facility, and although trace amounts of beryllium have been found on the grounds of two of these schools, the community has been told there is nothing to worry about (Child Proofing Our Communities Campaign, 2001; EPA, n.d.).

It is crucial to link these environmental conditions directly to the health and wellness of children throughout the United States (Lee, 2002). One of the most well-documented effects of negative environmental conditions on children is asthma, a disease with clear evidence of racial disparity.

Asthma

The medical community once thought asthma was a condition stemming solely from genetic predisposition; however, health professionals have determined that environmental conditions are the primary contributor to this medical condition (Brown et al., 2003). In light of this, it is not at all surprising that the data illustrate that children of color, who so often live in areas with toxic air, are much more likely to suffer from asthma than are their White counterparts. In a national study, 437 U.S. counties were determined to have air quality that fails to meet EPA standards. Figure 3.13 illustrates that 57% of the total U.S. White population lives in these counties, compared to 65% of the Black population and 80% of the Latino population (Bullard, 2005).

Furthermore, as depicted in Table 3.2, the American Lung Association determined that children of color are also more likely to live in areas that exceed national ozone standards. These ozone standards are

TABLE 3.2	
U.S. Children Living in Areas Exceeding Ozone Standards (Bullard, 2005)	
White	50.8%
Black	61.3%
Latino	69.2%
Asian	67.7%

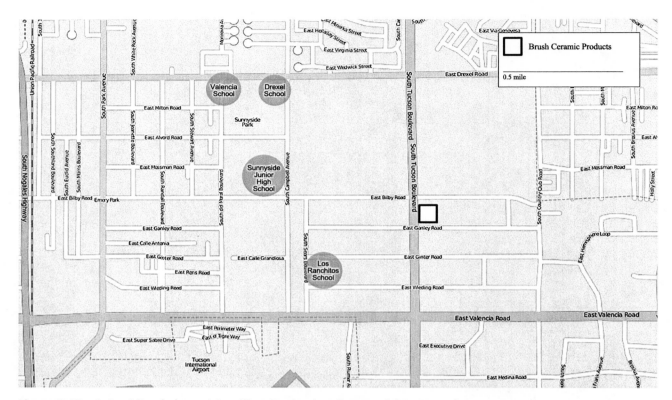

Figure 3.12   School Proximity and Beryllium Production, Tucson, Arizona

(EPA, n.d; © OpenStreetMap contributors, CC-BY-SA)

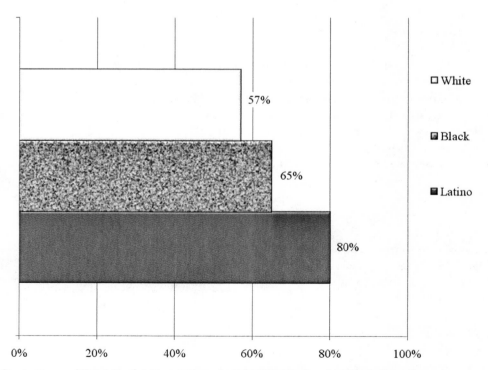

Figure 3.13   Percentage of Total Racial Populations in 437 EPA-Designated Toxic Counties

(Bullard, 2005)

TABLE 3.3
Asthma Prevalence Rates (American Lung Association, 2010)

	White 5- to 17-year-old children (rate per 1,000)	Black 5- to 17-year-old-children (rate per 1,000)	Percentage the Black population is higher than the White population in asthma prevalence
2001	139.4	170.8	22.5%
2002	132.6	183.5	38.4%
2003	134.6	184.8	37.3%
2004	129.0	196.9	52.6%
2005	134.0	182.7	36.3%
2006	151.1	192.7	27.5%
2007	134.7	210.6	56.3%
2008	147.7	252.3	70.8%

air pollution requirements for ozone, particulate matter, nitrogen oxides, carbon monoxide, sulfur dioxide, and lead set by the EPA (Bullard, 2005).

Given that the amount of pollution emitted in the United States has only increased over time, asthma has become the most prevalent childhood health condition in the nation. From 1980 through 1996, the number of asthmatics grew 73.9% to 14.6 million individuals. People of color and the poor experience a disproportionate share of this reality. These communities are 15–20% more likely than are Whites and those of higher SES to suffer from this respiratory condition (Brown et al., 2003). Examining the increase in asthma prevalence between White and Black children, the American Lung Association (2010) illustrates this disparity. The statistics in Table 3.3 detail the asthma prevalence rate in each population per every 1,000 children who were 5–17 years old from the years 2001–2008.

This sharp increase in the number of children diagnosed with asthma has prompted the medical community to work diligently to provide treatment and prevention education. However, as in the many examples highlighted in chapter 2, children of color often receive the least and/or worst treatment available. Studies have found that White children are more likely to receive regular treatment for asthma from a doctor's office, while Black children are more likely to have their symptoms go untreated until hospitalization is required (Lin, Pitt, Lou, & Yi, 2007; Moorman et al., 2007). Table 3.4 compiles data from a two-year study in New Jersey that found 1,384 more Black children than White children taken to the emergency

room for asthma. This means that Black children were more than three times more likely than White children to make such emergency room visits. Additionally, while the gross number of visits by Hispanic children is much lower than that of Whites, the nearly doubled rate in emergency room visits per 1,000 children exemplifies that their lower gross number is explained by their lower percentage of the overall population (Kruse, Deshpande, & Vezina, 2007).

Another study found that for every 1,000 children, 26.2 Black children went to the emergency room for asthma compared to nine White children (Akinbami & Schoendorf, 2002).

Many academics and researchers will argue that SES, not race, is responsible for the varying rates of asthma among White children and children of color. Some studies have investigated the data from a class perspective and, while being poor is never positive, race has been proven to be the more salient factor. When looking at the data, among "Black children . . . asthma prevalence was relatively level and high across income groups, resulting in a large racial/ethnic disparity among children in middle- to high-income families" (Miller, 2000, p. 429). To be poor and Black,

TABLE 3.4
Emergency Room Visits Due to Asthma
(Kruse et al., 2007)

	White	Black	Hispanic
Emergency Room Visits	14,730	16,114	9,290
Emergency Room Visits per every 1,000 children	4.7	16.1	8.8

as well as wealthy and Black, means that one has higher asthma prevalence and is more likely to be hospitalized than a White counterpart. These results have been duplicated in other research (Smith, Hatcher-Ross, Wertheimer, & Kahn, 2005). Such disparities for children of color also invariably affect mortality rates relating to asthma.

The death rate related to asthma has skyrocketed in every community. However, when looking at the entire White and Black population in the United States, we see marked increase in disparity. Figure 3.14 compares the mortality rates for Whites and Blacks using 1979 as the baseline. In that year, 2,095 Whites and 470 Blacks died due to asthma. The figure marks the percentage increase for each year when compared to the 1979 baseline.

As can be seen, the White population has experienced negative effects due to the widespread prevalence of asthma, with a 19.2% increase in their morbidity rate from 1979 to 2006, spiking in 1995

with a 100.9% difference from 1979. However, for Blacks with the same condition, that morbidity rate increased 103.6% from 1979 to 2006, reaching a summit in 1996 with a 181.9% increase (American Lung Association, 2010).

Another way to view the data is through age-adjusted death rates. These statistics use census information to estimate the asthma morbidity rate per 100,000 people in each population. In 2006, Whites died from asthma at a rate of 0.9 per every 100,000 people. For Blacks in 2006, that death rate was 2.7, three times higher (American Lung Association, 2010).

As for children, Figure 3.15 depicts that in 1997–1998, Black children with asthma were nearly 4.6 times more likely to die from asthma than White children (Akinbami & Schoendorf, 2002).

In an even more specific example, Chicago posts some of the highest asthma mortality rates in the country. The entire Black population in this city is eight

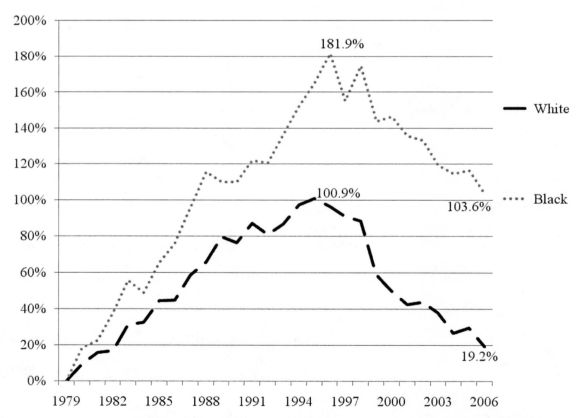

Figure 3.14   Increase in Asthma-Related Deaths With 1979 as Baseline for Comparison—Total Population

(American Lung Association, 2010)

times more likely to die from asthma than Whites. As for children under the age of 15, from 1992 to 2003, two White children died from this health condition. In the same time frame, 83 Black children died (Naureckas & Thomas, 2007).

Even those children who manage to live with this illness experience other ramifications. A notable example is the impact asthma can have on academic achievement. Mary Fowler, Marsha Davenport, and Rekha Garg (1992) examined the academic outcomes of students diagnosed with asthma, with several interesting results. Overall, children with asthma are nearly twice as likely to be diagnosed with a learning disability as children without asthma.

One possible explanation for the data in Table 3.5 may be that asthmatic children have a higher degree of absenteeism due to difficulty breathing, sleep irregularities, asthma attacks, and/or hospitalizations. Over

time, this will put them behind their peers and may lead some administrators to believe that they have a learning disability. We also know that asthma directly affects academic performance. Black and Hispanic students with asthma are much more likely to receive a failing grade when compared to White students with asthma. Lastly, Black students with asthma are four times more likely to be suspended or expelled from school than Whites with the same illness (see Figure 3.16; Fowler et al., 1992).

TABLE 3.5 Learning Disability and Asthma (Fowler et al., 1992)	
	Percentage of the Population Diagnosed With a Learning Disability
Children With Asthma	9%
Children Without Asthma	5%

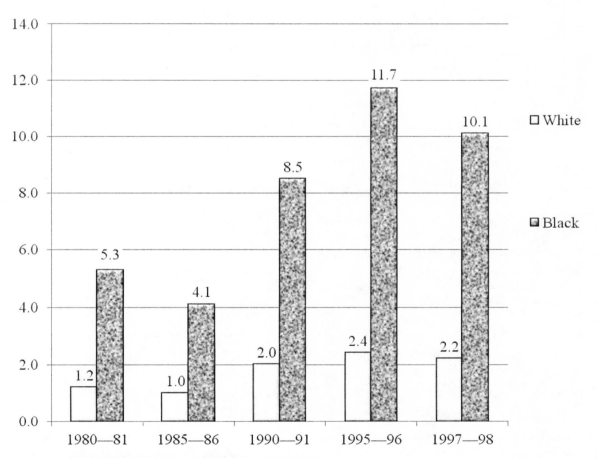

Figure 3.15 Child Mortality Rate for Asthma (per 1,000,000)

(Akinbami & Schoendorf, 2002)

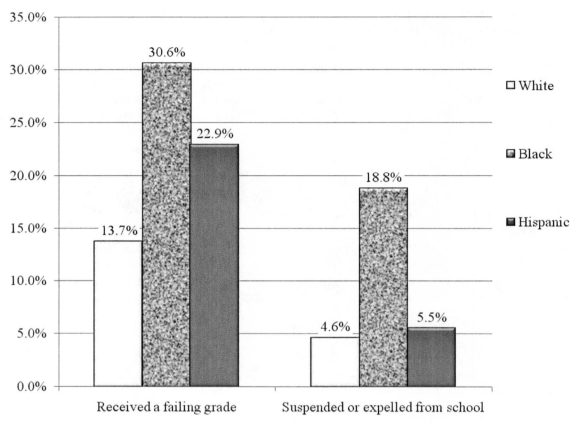

Figure 3.16   Academic Outcomes for Children Diagnosed With Asthma

(Fowler et al., 1992)

CONCLUSION

The diminished academic performance of those with asthma has nothing to do with intellectual aptitude. Their performance reflects the physical limitations of their health created by human-made pollution and exposure to toxins. While this chapter focuses mainly on the physical impact of this pollution and toxin exposure, there is an adjoined emotional element as well. Feeling ill, weak, and frail can negatively impact a child's self-confidence, thereby affecting many facets of life, including academic performance (Austin, Huberty, Huster, & Dunn, 1998). Furthermore, children's health issues affect the emotional well-being of parents (Brown et al., 2003; Maier, Arrighi, Morray, Llewllyn, & Redding, 1998). There is also evidence suggesting that parents of unhealthy children are likely to miss a great deal of work to care for their child, and this can affect a family's financial well-being, in addition to their physical and emotional health (Diette et al., 2000).

The data presented in these pages illustrate the severity of toxic environmental conditions as well as the encompassing negative effect they have on children. The research also demonstrates that families of color are much more likely to suffer environmental injustices than are their White counterparts.

REFERENCES

Akinbami, L. J., & Schoendorf, K. C. (2002). Trends in childhood asthma: Prevalence, health care utilization, and mortality. *Pediatrics, 110*(2), 315–322.

American Lung Association. (2010). *Trends in asthma morbidity and mortality.* Retrieved from http://www.lungusa.org/lung-disease/asthma/resources/

Next Steps for the Reader

- Use the EnviroMapper tool provided by the EPA to chart the pollution levels in your neighborhood. Compare your pollution exposure to the case studies detailed in chapter 3.
- Conduct an informal poll of your family, friends, and coworkers to see how many of them have asthma. Taking this a step further, ask how many of those with asthma regularly carry an inhaler.
- Inquire at your local elementary school about what types of cleaning products are used; when the last time a check for asbestos and mold was conducted; and about the quality of the heating, ventilation, and air conditioning system.

Additional Resources for Up-to-Date Facts and Stats

American Lung Association
- Asthma—http://www.lungusa.org/lung-disease/asthma/
- Asthma in Schools—http://www.lungusa.org/lung-disease/asthma/in-schools/
- State of Lung Disease in Diverse Communities—http://www.lungusa.org/finding-cures/our-research/solddc-index.html

EJnet.org: Web Resources for Environmental Justice Activists
- Homepage—http://www.ejnet.org/
- Environmental Justice / Environmental Racism—http://www.ejnet.org/ej/

Environmental Justice Resource Center at Clark Atlanta University
- Homepage—http://www.ejrc.cau.edu/

Scorecard: The Pollution Information Site
- Homepage—http://scorecard.goodguide.com/

U.S. Department of Transportation
- Environmental Justice—http://www.fhwa.dot.gov/environment/ej2.htm
- Nondiscrimination: Title VI and Environmental Justice—http://www.fhwa.dot.gov/environment/ejustice/facts/index.htm

U.S. Department of Transportation
- Environmental Justice—http://www.fhwa.dot.gov/environment/ej2.htm

U.S. Environmental Protection Agency
- Environmental Justice—http://www.epa.gov/environmentaljustice/
- EnviroMapper—http://www.epa.gov/emefdata/em4ef.home

Anderson, S. (2000). The school that wasn't: Politics and pollution in LA. *The Nation*, 32–36.

Ayrapetyan, E. (2010). Edward R. Roybal Learning Center [photograph]. Personal photo used with permission.

Austin, J. K., Huberty, T. J., Huster, G. A., & Dunn, D. W. (1998). Academic achievement in children with epilepsy or asthma. *Developmental Medicine & Child Neurology, 40*, 248–255.

Bowen, W. M., & Wells, M. V. (2002). The politics and reality of environmental justice: A history and considerations for public administrators and policy makers. *Public Administration Review, 62*(6), 688–698.

Brown, P., Mayer, B., Zavestoski, S., Luebke, T., Mandelbaum, J., & McCormick, S. (2003). The health politics of asthma: Environmental justice and collective illness experience in the United States. *Social Science & Medicine, 57*, 453–464.

Bullard, R. D. (1990). *Dumping in Dixie: Race, class and environmental quality.* Boulder, CO: Westview.

Bullard, R. D. (2005). Environmental justice in the twenty-first century. In R. D. Bullard (Ed.), *The quest for environmental justice: Human rights and the politics of pollution* (pp. 19–42). San Francisco: Sierra Club.

Bullard, R. D., Mohai, P., Saha, R., & Wright, B. (2007). *Toxic waste and race at twenty 1987–2007: Grassroots struggles to dismantle environmental racism in the United States.* Justice and Witness Ministries, United Church of Christ: Cleveland, OH. Retrieved from http://www.ucc.org/justice/pdfs/toxic20.pdf

Capek, S. M. (1993). The "environmental justice" frame: A conceptual discussion and application. *Social Problems, 40*(1), 5–24.

Chicago Public Schools. (2010). *Carver.* Retrieved from http://www.cps.edu/Schools/Pages/school.aspx?unit=2690

Child Proofing Our Communities Campaign. (2001). *Poisoned schools: Invisible threats, visible actions.* Falls Church, VA: Center for Health, Environment and Justice.

Cutter, S. L. (1995). Race, class and environmental justice. *Progress in Human Geography, 19*(1), 111–122.

Diette, G. B., Markson, L., Skinner, E. A., Nguyen, T. T. H., Algatt-Bergstrom, P., & Wu, A. W. (2000). Nocturnal asthma in children affects school attendance, school performance, and parents' work attendance. *Archives of Pediatrics and Adolescent Medicine, 154,* 923–928.

Downey, L. (1998). Environmental injustice: Is race or income a better predictor? *Social Science Quarterly, 79*(4), 766–778.

Environmental Protection Agency (EPA). (n.d.). *Enviro-Mapper for Envirofacts.* Retrieved from http://www.epa.gov/emefdata/em4ef.home

Executive Order No. 12898 (1994). Federal actions to address environmental justice in minority populations and low-income populations. *Federal Register, 59*(32). Retrieved from http://www.epa.gov/history/topics/justice/02.htm

Executive Order No. 13045. (1997). Protection of children from environmental health risks and safety risks. *Federal Register, 62*(78). Retrieved from http://www.epa.gov/fedreg/eo/eo13045.htm

FK1954. (2009). File: Carbon black.jpg. Retrieved from http://commons.wikimedia.org/wiki/File:Carbon_black.jpg#filehistory

Fowler, M. G., Davenport, M. G., & Garg, R. (1992). School functioning of US children with asthma. *Pediatrics, 90*(6), 939–944.

Hawthorne, M., & Little, D. (2008, September 28). Chicago's toxic air. *Chicago Tribune.* Retrieved from http://www.chicagotribune.com/news/local/chi-pollution-risk-29-se p29,0,4323308.story

Kruse, L. K., Deshpande, S., & Vezina, M. (2007). Disparities in asthma hospitalizations among children seen in the emergency department. *Journal of Asthma, 44*(10), 833–837.

Lee, C. (2002). Environmental justice: Building a unified vision of health and the environment. *Environmental Health Perspectives, 110*(2), 141–144.

Lin, R. Y., Pitt, T. J., Lou, W. Y., & Yi, Q. (2007). Asthma hospitalization patterns in young children relating to admission age, infection presence, sex, and race. *Annals of Allergy, Asthma and Immunology, 98*(2), 139–145.

Maier, W. C., Arrighi, M., Morray, B., Llewllyn, C., & Redding, G. J. (1998). The impact of asthma and asthma-like illness in Seattle school children. *Journal of Clinical Epidemiology, 51*(7), 557–568.

Masterton-Allen, S. B., & Brown, P. (1990). Public reaction to toxic waste contamination: Analysis of social movement. *International Journal of Health Services, 20,* 485–500.

Miller, J. E. (2000). The effects of race/ethnicity and income on early childhood asthma prevalence and health care use. *American Journal of Public Health, 90*(3), 428–430.

National Environment Trust, Physicians for Social Responsibility, and Learning Disabilities Association of America. (2000). *Polluting our future: Chemical pollution in the U.S. that affects child development and learning.* Retrieved from http://www.oztoxics.org/cmwg/library/documents_1/Polluting%20Our%20Future.pdf

Naureckas, E. T., & Thomas, S. (2007). Are we closing the disparities gap? *Chest, 132,* 858S–865S.

Norrell, B. (2005). Ponca file suit against carbon black company. *Indian Country Today, 24*(48), B1.

Northwest Coalition for Alternatives to Pesticides. (2000). *Unthinkable risk: How children are exposed and harmed when pesticides are used at school.* Eugene, OR: Northwest Coalition for Alternatives to Pesticides.

Pastor, M., Sadd, J. L., & Morello-Frosch, R. (2002). Who's minding the kids? Pollution, public schools, and environmental justice in Los Angeles. *Social Science Quarterly, 83*(1), 263–280.

Pellow, D. N. (2002). *Garbage wars: The struggle for environmental justice in Chicago.* Cambridge, MA: MIT Press.

People of Color Environmental Leadership Summit. (1991). *Principles of environmental justice.* New York:

United Church of Christ. Retrieved from http://www .ejnet.org/ej/principles.html

Pulido, L. (2000). Rethinking environmental racism: White privilege and urban development in Southern California. *Annals of the Association of American Geographers*, *90*(1), 12–40.

Resource Conservation and Recovery Act of 1976, 42 U.S.C. § 6901–6992k. (1976).

Roberts, J. T., & Toffolon-Weiss, M. M. (2001). *Chronicles from the environmental justice frontline*. Cambridge, UK: Cambridge University Press.

Sexton, K., & Adgate, J. L. (1999). Looking at environmental justice from an environmental health perspective. *Journal of Exposure and Environmental Epidemiology*, *9*, 3–8.

Shriver, T. E., & Webb, G. R. (2009). Rethinking the scope of environmental injustice: Perceptions of health hazards in rural Native American community exposed to carbon black. *Rural Psychology*, *74*(92), 270–292.

Smith, L. A., Hatcher-Ross, J. L., Wertheimer, R., & Kahn, R. S. (2005). Rethinking race/ethnicity, income, and childhood asthma: Racial/ethnic disparities concentrated among the very poor. *Public Health Reports*, *120*(2), 109–120.

Stewart, V. (2011). George Washington Carver Primary School [photograph]. Personal photo used with permission.

Suglia, S. F., Gryparis, A., Wright, R. O., Schwartz, J., & Wright, R. J. (2008). Association of black carbon with cognition among children in a prospective birth cohort study. *American Journal of Epidemiology*, *167*(3), 280–286.

Szaz, A. (1994). *Ecopopulism: Toxic waste and the movement for environmental justice*. Minneapolis: University of Minnesota Press.

United Church of Christ Commission for Racial Justice. (1987). *Toxic wastes and race in the United States: A national report on the racial and socio-economic characteristics of communities with hazardous waste sites*. New York: United Church of Christ.

United Nations. (1992). *Agenda 21: Programme of action for sustainable development*. New York: United Nations. Retrieved from http://www.un.org/documents/ga/ conf151/aconf15126–1annex1.htm

Wright, G. (2005). Living and dying in Louisiana's "Cancer Alley." In R. D. Bullard (Ed.), *The quest for environmental justice: Human rights and the politics of pollution* (pp. 87–107). San Francisco: Sierra Club.

4

Criminals or Children?
Juvenile Justice

With origins in Egyptian, Greek, and Roman folklore, a well-known figure in the United States is the statue of Lady Justice (depicted in Figure 4.1). Often adorning the fronts of courthouses, she holds weighted scales in one hand and a sword in the other, standing tall with a blindfold over her eyes. Having her eyes covered signifies that justice is blind and all are equal under the law. The scales and sword she holds "need not only remind us that Justice can be powerful and correct; they can also be interpreted as indications of Justice as harsh, unsympathetic, and un-yielding" (Curtis & Resnik, 1987, p. 1755).

Dissecting the meaning of this image serves as an il-luminating introduction to the topic of juvenile jus-tice. The mythology of our judicial system is that the "fair-and-balanced" review process ensures that all peo-ple receive their day in court. However, in a system run by fallible humans, it is impossible for these processes and outcomes to be free from biased opinions.

> The American criminal justice system is based on an interdependent relationship between impartial laws and culturally influenced legal agents; there-fore . . . the meaning of justice may depend on the social, economic, and cultural characteristics of the groups involved. (Cureton, 2000, p. 703)

Even though many believe laws are impartial, histori-cally this was often not the case and even today one can find evidence that not everyone is always treated

Figure 4.1   Lady Justice

(mikeoart.com, 2011)

equally in the eyes of the law. For example, competing cultural factors influence agents of our legal system, often victimizing children of color.

This chapter explores the stereotypical belief that people of color, in this case children, commit the majority of crime in our country. It also details how decisions are made during the judicial process for children of color and the racism that is often experienced at each level. Finally, I provide an overview of one state's efforts to improve this reality, detailing the progress made through a concerted effort.

THE MYTH IS WRONG

The stereotypical image of the juvenile offender as a child of color, more specifically Black, is a myth. Bluntly stated, White juveniles account for the vast majority of crime in the United States every single year. However, images of White juvenile offenders are rarely displayed in newspapers, on television news programs,

or on websites (Dorfman & Schiraldi, 2001). Figure 4.2 details these consistent crime statistics.

Figure 4.3 details nearly identical data collected five years later.

An omission in both data sets is information pertaining to Hispanics or Latina/os. The Federal Bureau of Investigation's (FBI) Uniform Crime Reporting (UCR) Program does not report data for this population because Hispanic is an ethnicity, not a race like White or Black. A person can be ethnically Hispanic and racially White. In fact, 90% of Hispanic juveniles in 2002 were White (Snyder & Sickmund, 2006). This problem of classification has led the UCR to steer clear of reporting anything regarding the population contemporary society would term Latina/o. It is noble that the FBI wants to ensure an accurate conceptualization of the difference between ethnicity and race. However, all researchers and government agencies need to recognize Latina/o as a racial category so we can accurately assess the needs of this growing population.

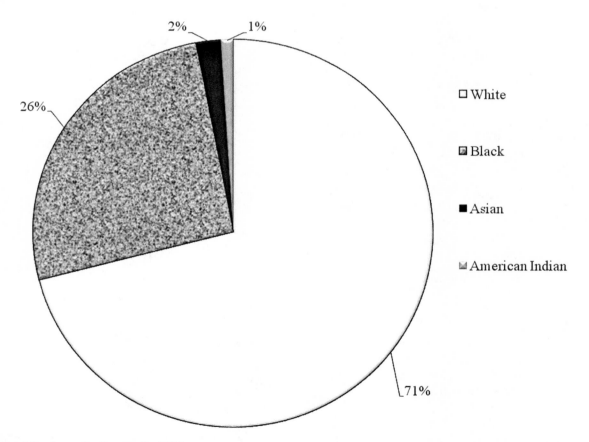

Figure 4.2   Juvenile Arrests in 1998

(Hawkins, Laub, Lauritsen, & Cothern, 2000)

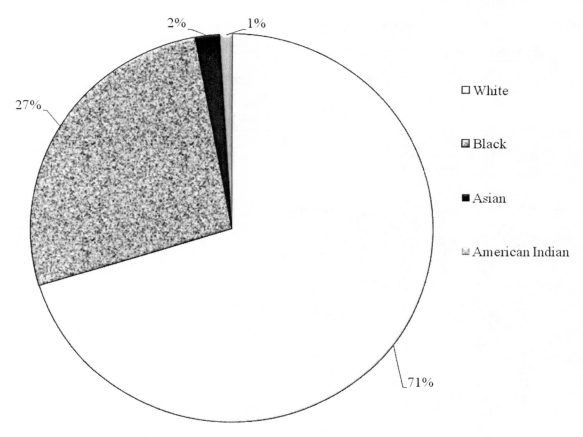

Figure 4.3 Juvenile Arrests in 2003

(Snyder & Sickmund, 2006)

In delving deeper into juvenile arrest records, we find White violent crime has skyrocketed in recent decades. For example, from 1983 to 1992, the violent crime arrest rate increased 82% for White juveniles. Over the same period, it increased by 43% for Black juveniles (Hawkins et al., 2000). Table 4.1 highlights several other noteworthy trends in the statistics detailing crimes committed when delineated by race.

TABLE 4.1				
Statistics for Juvenile Crime Delineated by Race (Snyder & Sickmund, 2006)				
	White	*Black*	*American Indian*	*Asian*
Murder/Nonnegligent Manslaughter	49%	48%	1%	2%
Rape	64%	33%	2%	1%
Aggravated Assault	59%	38%	1%	1%
Total Property Crime Index	69%	28%	1%	2%
Weapons	66%	32%	1%	2%
Sex Offense	71%	26%	1%	1%
Drugs	72%	26%	1%	1%
Driving Under the Influence	94%	4%	2%	1%
Disorderly Conduct	64%	34%	1%	1%
Curfew/Loitering	68%	30%	1%	1%

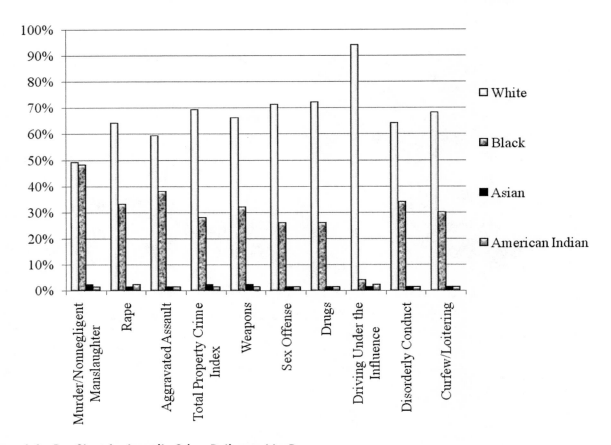

Figure 4.4   Bar Chart for Juvenile Crime Delineated by Race

(Snyder & Sickmund, 2006)

Figure 4.4 assists in making meaning of the data-heavy information in Table 4.1.

Though common stereotypes seem to elicit fear of Black youth, statistically it makes more sense to be fearful of Whites. White youth constitute the majority of arrests, and in rape and drunk driving the disparity is great. According to the National Highway Traffic Safety Administration (2008), drunk driving alone accounted for 12,998 deaths in 2007; Table 4.1 details that White juveniles were responsible for 94% of the youth arrests for this offense. Furthermore, the FBI (2008) reported that in 2007 there were 90,427 rapes in the United States. While this number is high, it represents only a fraction of the number of sexual assaults, as rape is one of the most underreported crimes. Regardless, White youths constituted 64% of rape arrests for juveniles.

My point in highlighting these facts is not to isolate White youth as particularly deviant. Rather, I hope to debunk the myth that youth of color are the sole or likely perpetrators of crime. Even in the case of murder, the statistics are even between Whites and Blacks.

Research has worked to unravel the complex social conditions that draw youth to crime. Nonetheless, as will be exemplified, we cannot deny that police arrest youth of color at disproportionate rates. There are a number of reasons for this imbalance. A major section of this chapter is devoted to the various decision points (e.g., police contact, arrest, adjudication) made in the juvenile justice system that reflect embedded racism, but there are still other factors, including how race and class come together to explain children's propensity toward or away from crime. Table 4.2 reveals this interaction.

These statistics are highly instructive, but not simple to comprehend at first glance. First, it is important to consider the coding structure. When researchers surveyed participants, their answers were placed into

	Had physical fight in last 6 months	Used alcohol, marijuana, or cocaine in last month	Parents have college degree	Family annual income
White	.26	.40	.29	$47,170
Asian	.21*	.26*	.36*	$50,530
American Indian	.41*	.33	.10*	$27,750*
Black	.36*	.19*	.16*	$26,090*
Latino	.28	.34*	.11*	$27,690*

TABLE 4.2 Juvenile Behaviors, Race, and SES (McNulty & Bellair, 2003)

* Statistically significant from White population ($p < .05$).

various categories labeled with either a 0 or a 1. These categories are as follows:

- Had physical fight in last 6 months: 0 = no; 1 = yes
- Used alcohol, marijuana, or cocaine in last month: 0 = no; 1 = yes
- Parents attended some college: 0 = no; 1 = yes
- Parents have college degree: 0 = no; 1 = yes
- Family annual income: this is reported in dollars earned per year (McNulty & Bellair, 2003)

From there, researchers totaled the scores, calculated an average for each racial group, and completed another computation to determine the results.

Every racial group reported, at some level, being in a fight in the last six months, with American Indian and Black youths reporting higher rates that are statistically significant ($p < .05$) when compared to White youths. Comparing this with the measures of social capital, parental education, and annual income, these children of color were at the bottom across the board. Such a low social standing not only affects the neighborhoods these children live in, it also determines the resources in their community. These results support the argument that the lower social standing of children of color significantly affects their views on violence. Struggle is inevitable in these neighborhoods, forcing children to fight to survive (McNulty & Bellair, 2003).

The drug and alcohol data in Table 4.2 raise an interesting discussion. Although society is more likely to label children of color as problem children, White juveniles are statistically more likely to drink and do drugs, to a statistically significant amount, in every

group save one (McNulty & Bellair, 2003). Perhaps these are viewed as victimless crimes, that is, until they get behind the wheel of a car (see data on driving under the influence in Table 4.1). What all of these statistics prove is that it is time to revisit our views on juvenile delinquency issues and question the mythologies that guide much of the contemporary discourse.

DECISION POINTS IN THE JUVENILE JUSTICE SYSTEM

Decision points in the juvenile justice system are those instances where choices are made about the path a child will follow. For instance, when police make contact with a child in regard to an alleged crime, the officer makes a choice whether to arrest or let the child go with a warning. Examining such decision points throughout the juvenile justice system is crucial. Racism creates a cumulative negative effect that snowballs as we send youth of color through the judicial system (Poe-Yamagata & Jones, 2005). We can conceptualize this phenomenon as a life-course perspective.

The life-course perspective is often used in sociologic research. It attributes, for instance, the higher incidences of Black juveniles in the court system to a variety of factors, such as interaction with child welfare, witnessing violence, being victimized themselves, police harassment, and judicial bias (Center for Juvenile Justice Reform, 2008; Shaffer & Ruback, 2002). Even exposure to racism from an early age can have severe negative consequences over the long term. The following list details children's experiences of racism:

- 67% reported racist insults;
- 46% had been called a racist slur;
- 33% were withheld from an opportunity due to race;
- 18% were threatened physically due to their race;
- 54% had friends victimized due to race; and
- 48% had family victimized due to race (Simons, Chen, Stewart, & Brody, 2003).

These instances, especially for boys, are linked to delinquency. Fear, anger, and other intense emotions are difficult to handle and can cause children to act violently as a measure of self-protection (Simons et al., 2003).

The life-course perspective attributes the sum total of such formative experiences as an explanatory factor for the present-day social conditions of people (Center for Juvenile Justice Reform, 2008; Shaffer & Ruback, 2002). This explains not only negative life results, but positive ones as well. Living in a gated community with access to adequate health care, safe schools, and free from hate assaults and crimes will lead to more positive outcomes. Children, however, do not get to pick where they are born; they must play the cards they are dealt.

The following review of decision points in the judicial process offers only a singular snapshot of a child's life course, but the data speak volumes.

Decision Point #1—Arrest

This is the most difficult aspect of juvenile justice to write about for two reasons. First, researchers in this area have had difficulty creating viable data sets because much police work is difficult to quantify. There are exact statistics for arrests and charges, but the data relating to those who were apprehended but let go are much more difficult to find (McCord, Spatz Widom, & Cromwell, 2001). As Alex Piquero states, "The police are a critical part of the decision-making system and are afforded far more discretion than any other formal agent of social control" (2008, p. 69). Second, while there was research several decades ago pointing toward racist actions by police, the more recent results are mixed. While this might relate to the aforementioned difficulty in gathering data, it may also indicate that the problem has improved. From the passage of laws such as the Juvenile Justice and Delinquency Prevention Act, as well as many state initiatives, police to-

day are "better educated and more diverse," and the training they receive may have improved "the attitudes and values that police officers bring to their work" (McCord et al., 2001, p. 245). However, there are still enough problems present to warrant further consideration, especially since racism in juvenile arrest decisions has the ability to permeate the entire system of justice (Piquero, 2008). The damage done at the beginning of the process has the ability to create systemic "cumulative disadvantage" whereby children of color will be affected by one racist system after another (Poe-Yamagata & Jones, 2005, p. 158).

There is significantly more data regarding arrest decisions with adults than with children. For example, one study found that when Blacks live in a city that is governed largely by Whites, Black citizens are more likely to be arrested, even when variables such as type of crime and SES are held constant (Cureton, 2000). Other research has found that police respond more quickly to calls from affluent areas than to those areas lower in SES (McCord et al., 2001). Nonetheless, even though there is less literature on juveniles, present data found that police officers are more likely to arrest juveniles than adults for the same crime. Therefore, the judicial system is more likely to affect individuals earlier in their life (Mastrofski, Worden, & Snipes, 1995).

One study examining children and arrests across five separate counties reported a statistically significant difference in arrest rates by race ($p < .001$). Holding race as a dependent variable, the researchers found a $-.30$ correlation between the race of an individual and the arrest decision. This means that when the alleged suspect was White, that suspect had a lower likelihood of arrest when in contact with police. Conversely, people of color had a much higher likelihood of arrest following police contact. Cumulatively, Black children account for 67% of all arrests made across the five separate counties in the study. Many argue that this population simply breaks the law more often. However, even when other important factors were included for consideration, such as weapons, drugs, and prior arrests, race was still a statistically significant factor in arrests (Wordes, Bynum, & Corley, 1994).

Other research has attempted to delve deeper into this issue by including gender and SES as variables along with race.

Researchers define police contact as the number of instances police officers interact with a person, whether

TABLE 4.3
Juvenile Contact With Police
(Sealock & Simpson, 1998)

	Overall Police Contact Percentage
White, Female, High SES	3.8%
White, Female, Low SES	2.3%
White, Male, High SES	13.2%
White, Male, Low SES	7.5%
Black, Female, High SES	2.8%
Black, Female, Low SES	11.6%
Black, Male, High SES	11.4%
Black, Male, Low SES	47.3%

through a criminal investigation or questioning. The data in Table 4.3 are too old to make significant projections, since they cover the years from 1968 to 1975. However, they set a baseline for the much greater likelihood of police contact if you are a person of color, male, and of lower SES as opposed to White, female, and of a higher SES. These differences are statistically significant ($p < .001$) (Sealock & Simpson, 1998).

Looking at this topic in yet another manner, Simon Singer (1996) examined police decisions for juvenile felony arrests. This classification sorts crimes according to classes where Class A represents the worst possible crimes and Class C covers lesser crimes. For example, a Class A felony would be murder, a Class B would be rape or manslaughter, and a Class C would be a simple burglary or assault.

Data from New York State show that police are more likely to arrest Black children for less serious offenses. White and Hispanic juveniles commit Class C felonies as well, but the data in Table 4.4 illustrate that police officers are less tolerant of Black juveniles. Remember, whether or not to arrest is a *decision* a police officer must make; an arrest does not simply happen

TABLE 4.4
Felony Classification, Race, and the Decision to Arrest (Singer, 1996)

	Class A Felony	Class B Felony	Class C Felony
White	9%	65%	27%
Black	5%	60%	35%
Hispanic	8%	66%	26%

automatically once a person breaks the law. For Class A felonies, the White juvenile arrest rate was nearly double that of Black juveniles. In these instances, police cannot ignore the serious crimes committed by White juveniles. Meanwhile, the public perception of the violent Black youth continues (Singer, 1996).

Accompanying these data is another set of numbers that almost appear contradictory. For the entire state of New York, race was a statistically significant predictor of the severity of the charge levied against youth ($p < .05$). In other words, police were more likely to arrest Black juveniles for serious offenses than they were Whites. How does one make sense of this in light of the data that say that Whites have the highest arrest percentage of Class A felons? The answer lies in the cumulative judicial process. Since police arrest Black juveniles more often in the Class C category, any of their future arrests, even minor ones, increase the severity of the charge. This is proof positive of a bias in the system that discriminates against Black children cumulatively over time (Singer, 1996).

Adding another scholarly dimension, Darlene Conley (1994) completed extensive qualitative research to understand the experience of youth of color prior to arrest. When asked for their perceptions on criminal activity, one child said, "The cops are everywhere. They've been messing with you so long, it's like, you know, fuck it, I don't care no more" (p. 141). This sentiment was reflected in an interview with an outreach worker who said, "The kids say that if they are going to get harassed by the police, they might as well be doing something" (Conley, 1994, p. 141). With disproportionate police contact, arrest rates, and felony classifications for those arrests, it is not difficult to understand the sentiments of these children.

Others from within the judicial system are willing to admit there is racism in arrest decisions. The following is an excerpt from an interview with a prosecutor. Researchers asked this individual to explain why there is racial disparity in arrests. The prosecutor readily admits that there are other factors under consideration.

Prosecutor: Because the police departments selectively enforce laws. I've been told that by police officers. That they have been told in these certain towns to look the other way, to take the [White] kids who are caught doing drugs home to their parents with a stern warning. . . . (Kupchik, 2006, p. 142)

Such flexibility is not often bestowed on youth of color. If police officers are "influenced by fear" and believe youth of color are "poor, unemployed, on welfare, less educated, dangerous, and poor risks for rehabilitation," then, of course, that is going to affect their decision-making processes (Leiber, 2003, p. 37). Such a dynamic will set youths against police, creating an antagonistic relationship even before their first interaction.

Decision Point #2—Intake

One might believe that following arrest, the judicial process is linear, a clear path with procedural steps at each point, but this is far from the truth. Intake is another decision point on the path a child may follow. In 2003 alone, 20% of children arrested never made it past the police department. Once children are taken into the station, agents of the justice system may create what the judicial system refers to as an informal remedy. This could include restitution to the victim, drug treatment, or informing the parents. These options constitute quite a favorable outcome for the children in question because, in such cases, their record remains clear (Snyder & Sickmund, 2006). However, 70% of children taken in are referred to juvenile court, and another 9% are sent to adult criminal proceedings (Puzzanchera, 2009). This decision point marks another instance where being a child of color has an effect on the outcome.

When the case is still in the police officers' hands, and they have decided not to involve parents or release the child, there are two additional options. The first, diversion, is an agreement made between the child and the juvenile system that the child will complete a program such as drug treatment. If the child complies, the justice system never files formal charges. Option two is to proceed with charges against the youth in court. In a study encapsulating four separate jurisdictions in Iowa, we find a racist precedent in each area. The statistics in Table 4.5 for diversion and court do not equal 100% because the remaining statistics constitute juve-

niles who were released into the custody of parents or released outright.

Racial disparities for diversion are seen across Table 4.5. In Bond alone, the judicial system grants Whites diversion at rates 11 percentage points higher than Blacks and sends Whites to court at rates 9 percentage points lower (Leiber, 2003). Figure 4.5 reports similar results from a book, entitled *Our Children, Their Children*.

These data show the advantage of being White, even in court referrals.

If the decision is made to send a child to court, judicial authorities then need to decide whether the child will be released from custody prior to those proceedings or held until a hearing before a judge. Figure 4.6 reports the probabilities for the judicial system detaining a child until court, with both race and gender as mitigating factors.

An interaction effect in detainment clearly exists between race and gender. Being female appears to have an effect on this decision point, bringing more males to detention centers. In addition, in both categories, being a youth of color means that you are much more likely to be kept in custody. For males, 13 percentage points separate the racial groups (Guevara, Herz, & Spohn, 2006). As detailed in Table 4.6, these results find support in other publications.

Other research has taken such investigations beyond Black and White youths; one researcher investigated racial disparities between Whites and Native Americans in a Wisconsin county (Poupart, 1995) (see Figure 4.7).

These statistics run parallel to the previous research. A 24 percentage point gap in juvenile court referral and a 7.1 percentage point gap in detention prior to that court date between Whites and Native Americans raise serious concerns (Poupart, 1995).

Another research study found that when Whites were in trouble for drugs, they were less likely to be detained than other offenders. For Blacks, there was a statistically significant 10% increase in detainment

	TABLE 4.5 Outcomes Following Arrest in Four Iowa Counties (Leiber, 2003)							
	Parks		*King*		*Jackson*		*Bond*	
	White	*Black*	*White*	*Black*	*White*	*Black*	*White*	*Black*
Diversion	59%	56%	33%	24%	70%	58%	55%	44%
Court	28%	31%	15%	19%	13%	16%	33%	42%

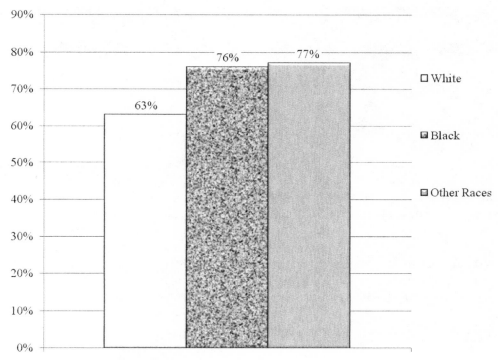

Figure 4.5   Juveniles Referred to Court Following Arrest

(Hawkins & Leonard, 2005)

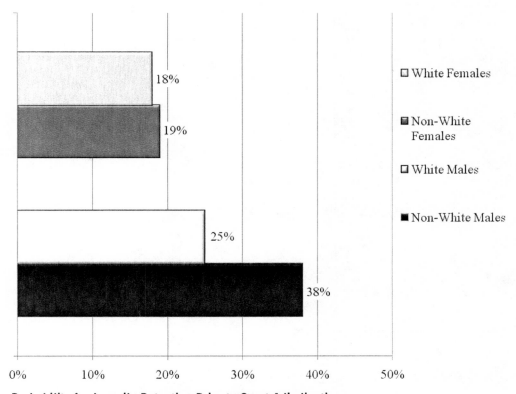

Figure 4.6   Probability for Juvenile Detention Prior to Court Adjudication

(Guevara, Herz, & Spohn, 2006)

TABLE 4.6 Juveniles Detained Between Arrest and Court (Hawkins & Leonard, 2005)	
	Detained Between Arrest and Court
White	18%
Black	25%
Other races	23%

TABLE 4.7 White Juvenile Correlation (Guevara et al., 2006)	
	White Juvenile Correlation
Detained prior to court	−.255
Received out-of-home placement following court	−.096

when arrested for drugs. In another finding, White children from a single-parent home had a 6% greater likelihood of being released prior to court than did their Black counterparts. For Black children in the exact same circumstance, there was a 6% increase in their confinement (Leiber & Fox, 2005). These results raise numerous questions regarding perceived severity of drug offenses by minors and potential assumptions legal authorities make about the home lives of children with single parents.

There is a final important two-part takeaway to this section derived from the data in Table 4.7.

First, the previously presented statistics reflecting racism in detention decisions gain further support in the correlation of children detained prior to court. This statistic was computed by coding the youths as either White or non-White (children of color). White juveniles had a statistically significant ($p \leq .05$) negative correlation with the likelihood of being detained prior to their court case. The juvenile justice system was more likely to detain children of color. These data interact meaningfully with the second important factor regarding judicial outcomes. White juveniles were less likely to receive out-of-home placement (e.g.,

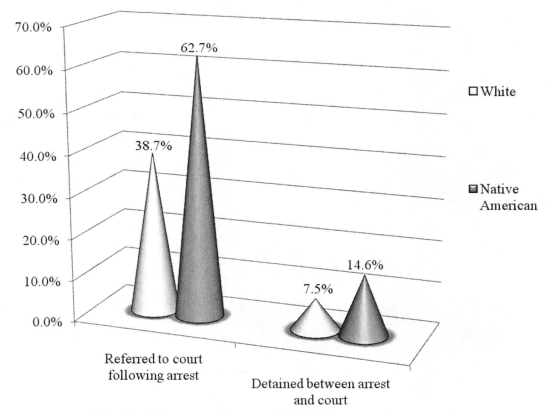

Figure 4.7   Juvenile Justice Racial Differences, White and Native American

(Poupart, 1995)

serve time in a juvenile detention facility) following court proceedings. This difference was also statistically significant ($p < .05$). As reported in the research, "being detained prior to the adjudication hearing nearly tripled the chances of out-of-home placement for non-White males . . . [and] this is compounded by the fact that they were substantially more likely than other youth to be detained in the first place" (Guevara et al., 2006, p. 275).

Decision Point #3—Adjudication and Disposition

Adjudication and disposition, the final steps in the juvenile justice system, follow arrest and intake. These steps occur in the court as children, represented by an attorney, stand before a judge and receive a sentence. At each step, statistics illustrate that racism permeates the decision points, leading ultimately to judges placing Black youths in juvenile correctional institutions at a rate 4.6 times higher than their similarly situated White peers (Feld, 1999). The Office of Juvenile Justice and Delinquency Prevention released the statistics about children held in institutions seen in Table 4.8.

TABLE 4.8	
Number of Juveniles in Residential Placement (per 100,000) (Sickmund, 2004)	
White	212
Black	1,004
Hispanic	485
Native American	632
Asian	182

But, before children can receive a sanction as shown in Table 4.8, they must seek assistance from their legal counsel.

Receiving effective legal counsel, something required by law, is not a given. The Federal Advisory Committee on Juvenile Justice (FACJJ) reported, "Lawyers are appointed or assigned to represent indigent youth in a startling low percentage of cases; moreover, this impacts disproportionately on lower income minority juveniles" (2006, p. 31). And for those children who do receive legal representation, they often do not meet with the lawyer at all before the proceedings. The lawyer simply meets them in the courtroom seconds before the process begins. In defense of these attorneys, this reality is not due to mali-

cious intent. Rather, they typically have full caseloads and no resources to assist their clients beyond their time in the courtroom (FACJJ, 2008). This issue with legal counsel is particularly problematic for children of color. Michael Leiber and Kristan Fox (2005) found that when both Black and White youth were not provided a lawyer, the Black youth were 17 percentage points more likely to receive a harsher judicial sanction than the White youth.

Judges have the sole discretion to determine an outcome that may radically alter a child's life forever. True to the philosophy of the juvenile system, if judges have individual discretion about the disposition of a juvenile case, they can individually tailor decisions addressing the needs of children. While an admirable goal, this is not how the system actually operates. In rural contexts, this individualized justice may come closer to fruition because these systems tend to have a lower caseload and are more informal. It is worthy of note that the more rural a community is, the more White it is likely to be. However, for urban jurisdictions, the exact opposite is true. The high caseload, alongside a greater amount of outside scrutiny, has brought forth an increasingly uniformed process (Feld, 1995). Another writer expressed fear of such a standardized system:

> I am concerned that any prescribed system of mandatory, graduated sanctions that is based solely on the nature and number of juvenile offenses, without taking into account the juvenile's history and stage development, will impede the justice system's ability to respond intelligently and with appropriate flexibility. (Carnell, 2005, p. 123)

Nonetheless, this dynamic is what we have; urban courts tend to dispense more severe, unvarying sanctions than their rural counterparts.

This creates a two-part problem for children of color. First, a large percentage of people of color live in urban metropolises. Second, since children of color have an increased likelihood of being arrested and referred to court, they will stand before uniformed judges who may sanction an offense severely. Conversely, a White youth living in a rural town has increased odds of receiving a preferential judicial outcome.

In exploring potential judicial decisions, the most promising outcome for any offender is to have his or her case dismissed. A dismissal not only ends the process, it allows the person to return to regular life. As shown in Figure 4.8, however, children of color are 9% less likely to get such a favorable outcome (Singer, 1996).

Remember, as outlined in this chapter, Whites are more likely to be arrested. Yet, these same youth are more likely to have their cases dismissed, leading to an overall lower conviction rate. The conviction rate is 7% for White juvenile offenders and 10% for Latina/o and Black juvenile offenders. The data in Figure 4.9 reveal that once one is convicted, race again affects the outcomes.

For these children of color, this represents a statistically significant disparity. They stand a 1.71 times greater chance of being securely detained in comparison to Whites. This statistic remains significant, even when controlled for the judicial infraction (Singer, 1996). These results, illustrating the same racial disparity, have been replicated in other research (Snyder & Sickmund, 2006) (see Table 4.9).

Research has broken these statistics down in another manner as well by looking for a correlative dif-

TABLE 4.9 Juvenile Conviction Outcomes in Drug Offense Cases (Snyder & Sickmund, 2006)		
	White	*Black*
Dismissed before reaching court	13.3%	8.4%
Placed in a public/private facility following adjudication	5.9%	13.3%

ference in judicial outcome according to race. First, researchers detailed a positive correlation of .161 between being a White juvenile and receiving probation as a sanction. This correlation was statistically significant ($p \leq .05$) (Guevara et al., 2006). Research published two years later reported a correlation between race and receiving out-of-home placement following a court case. In this instance the correlation was negative, −.096, for White juveniles being placed outside of their home following conviction. Again, this correlation represents a statistically significant difference ($p \leq .05$) (Guevara, Herz, & Spohn, 2008).

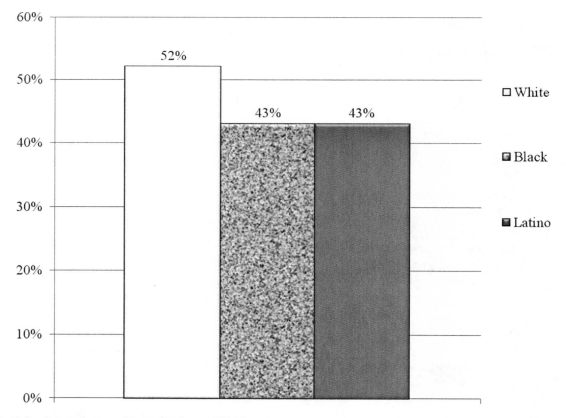

Figure 4.8   Percentages of Juvenile Cases Dismissed

(Singer, 1996)

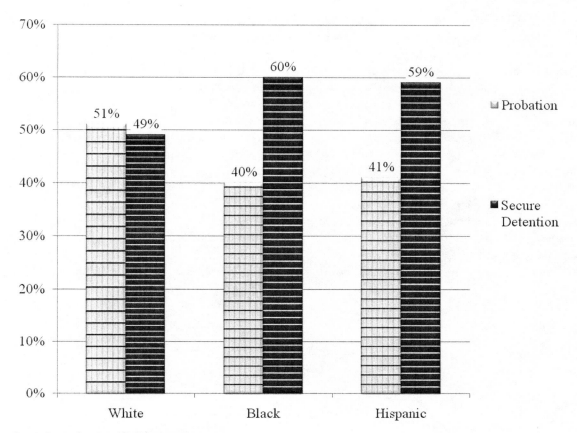

Figure 4.9   Juvenile Conviction Outcomes

(Singer, 1996)

In another study in Pennsylvania, researchers reported that Latina/os and Blacks were more likely to receive harsher sentencing, such as residential placement, than their White peers. On the other hand, White youths had options such as private care facilities and substance abuse treatment centers (Kempf Leonard & Sontheimer, 1995). This racial difference can also include differentials in that more-affluent Whites may have the parental income or health insurance to cover these preferential sanction options.

The most likely argument to deflect this charge of racism is that perhaps these statistics are ignoring other factors such as previous arrests. But, as the following study details, even when previous arrest records are taken into account, racism still affects outcomes. In Hennepin County, Minnesota, which includes Minneapolis, a researcher investigated racial differences between youths convicted of a felony upon a person and their prescribed sanction. The sanctions were out-of-home confinement or secure lockup. These statistics were split by the youths' prior arrest record, as reported in Table 4.10.

TABLE 4.10 Juvenile Conviction Sanctions for Felony Committed Upon a Person, Prior Criminal History (Feld, 1995)				
	White		*Black*	
	0 priors	*1–2 priors*	*0 priors*	*1–2 priors*
Out-of-home confinement	44.4%	27.3%	55.6%	50.0%
Secure lockup	35.2%	18.2%	47.2%	44.4%

As detailed in Table 4.10, race had more of an effect on judicial outcomes than did prior arrest. Just by examining the repeat offenders, there is a 22.7 percentage point difference in receiving out-of-home confinement in favor of White juveniles and a 26.2 percentage point difference in being sent to a secure lockup in favor of Black juveniles. Additionally, when these outcomes are computed for Black and Native American youth in comparison to Whites, there is a statistically significant difference between these groups in both regards ($p < .01$ Black/White; $p < .05$ Native American/White) (Feld, 1995).

For a final peek inside these numbers, one set of researchers (McCord et al., 2001) compiled a data set and associated graphic (Figure 4.10) to exemplify this cumulative racial disparity and its differential effects on children.

Each box enumerates the White and Black juveniles interacting with each step of the judicial process. In addition, stemming out from each population on the top and bottom of the figure is the probability that those juveniles will interact with that step of the judicial process. For the entire Black youth population, the probability they will end up in a juvenile residential facility at some point is .0053 or .53%. For White youth the research identified their probability at .0017 or .17%. This is a more than three times greater likelihood for Black youth to enter a juvenile residential facility. Furthermore, other data denote that after arrest and court sentencing, 32% of Black juveniles are placed in a residential facility, compared to only 26% for White children. This six percentage point disparity highlights systemic racial disparity in judicial outcomes (McCord et al., 2001).

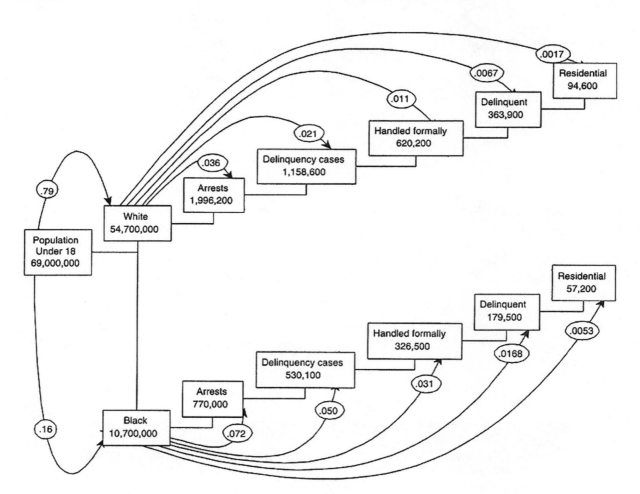

Figure 4.10   Compounding of Risk Through Judicial System, by Race

(McCord et al., 2001) [Reprinted with permission from the National Academics Press, Copyright 2001, National Academy of Sciences]

CASE STUDY—WASHINGTON STATE

Washington State has made a concerted effort to address the disproportionate minority contact (DMC) in its judicial processes. The state took a three-step approach. First, it did its own research, partnering with academics throughout the state. Second, it wrote legislation stemming from the recommendations put forth in the research. And last, it enacted programming through the legislation to address this problem (Hsia, Bridges, & McHale, 2004).

In beginning its research, the Washington legislature enlisted the help of state agencies, the University of Washington, and the Governor's Juvenile Justice Advisory Committee (GJJAC). The GJJAC became the leader of the project (Hsia et al., 2004). It interviewed justice department officials, rode along in police cars, traced court cases from police contact through disposition, and examined the role of the probation officer. In each instance, the results further supported the data presented in this chapter:

> Minority youth were more likely than whites to be referred, detained, prosecuted, adjudicated, and confined in juvenile correctional facilities, and at rates higher than would be expected given their numbers in the population. (Hsia et al., 2004, p. 20).

These children of color were also more likely to have negative evaluations from probation officers based on judgments regarding persona and character.

In response to these findings, four pieces of legislation were enacted. Engrossed Substitute House Bill 1966, passed in 1993, mandated that any county seeking state funding must create measures to address DMC. Furthermore, this bill called on justice officials to review their procedures to address the disparate courtroom outcomes. House Bill 2319 from 1994 required every juvenile court in the state to monitor and appraise racial inequality. It also created local councils in each county to assist in the juvenile court supervision of this issue. In 1996, the legislature passed House Bill 2392, which set up a trial program in two counties to address DMC. These programs were assessed holistically and provided recommendations for statewide implementation. Last, Engrossed Substitute House Bill 3900, also known as the Juvenile Accountability Act, was passed in 1997. This act brought together government agencies to collaborate in creating guidelines for community-driven initiatives to address DMC. Alongside this initiative, court personnel wrote the Washington Association of Juvenile Court Administrators-Risk Assessment. This tool put forth a well-thought-out evaluation of youth in contact with juvenile courts in hopes of reducing bias-influenced decisions (Hsia et al., 2004).

All four of these laws established a solid foundation to diminish DMC. For instance, funding helped to create comprehensive diversity trainings for state officials; police officers, lawyers, judges, and probation officers were all eligible to receive instruction and development. New initiatives also continued assessment of this phenomenon. And, finally, tools like the aforementioned Washington Association of Juvenile Court Administrators-Risk Assessment continued to be developed. These initiatives, programs, and tools are invaluable additions in meeting the needs of children in the juvenile justice system (Hsia et al., 2004).

Measuring change is the final important piece of this case study. We need to see whether these steps made any difference at all in decreasing DMC. Table 4.11

TABLE 4.11
Washington State: Youth of Color in the Juvenile Justice System (Hsia et al., 2004)

Youth of Color Percentages in Juvenile Justice System			
	1990	*1999*	*Percentage Point Difference 1999–1990*
Received diversion	22.6%	25.7%	3.1
Held at least 24 hours before court	48.5%	38.6%	−9.9
Sent to court	35.8%	33.6%	−2.2
Found responsible for violating law	32.1%	31.7%	−0.4
Court judgment included juvenile detention	30.6%	33.2%	2.6

gives a few statistics from 1990 and 1999 detailing the difference.

Most of these numbers show improvement in the experience children of color have with the Washington justice system. After 10 years of work, there was a 3.1 percentage point increase in the number of children of color receiving diversion programs instead of court adjudication. In addition, there was a 9.9 percentage point decrease in pretrial detention and a 2.2 percentage point decrease in children of color sent to court. While incredibly small, there was a decrease in children found responsible for breaking the law in a court process. These numbers are far from satisfactory, but the progress is hopeful (Hsia et al., 2004).

CONCLUSION

While the statistics in this chapter reveal a great deal about racism in the juvenile justice system, one other point worth mentioning is language. In compiling resources for this book, this is the only chapter where the language in the research shifted from using the terms youths, children, or kids to the use of the term juveniles. While the term juvenile technically pertains to the young, it also carries with it a secondary, pejorative quality. It ascribes judgment to those pesky *juveniles* who crowd our courtrooms and are supported by our tax dollars in *juvenile* facilities throughout the country. The language we use creates a viewpoint from which we operate. When we stop viewing the young who violate the law as children, we run astray from the mission of the justice system. For children, this system should promote healthy decision making and equal treatment under the law.

REFERENCES

Carnell, L. H. (2005). Harsh punishment is not the best way to prevent juvenile crime. In A. C. Nakaya (Ed.), *Juvenile crime: Opposing viewpoints* (pp. 121–125). Farmington Hills, MI: Greenhaven.

Center for Juvenile Justice Reform. (2008). *Racial and ethnic disparity and disproportionality in child welfare and juvenile justice: A compendium.* Washington DC: Georgetown Public Policy Institute. Retrieved from http://cjjr.georgetown.edu/pdfs/cjjr_ch_final.pdf

Conley, D. J. (1994). Adding color to a black and white picture: Using qualitative data to explain racial disproportionality in the juvenile justice system. *Journal of Research in Crime and Delinquency, 31*(2), 135–148.

Cureton, S. R. (2000). Justifiable arrests or discretionary justice: Predictors of racial arrest differentials. *Journal of Black Studies, 30*(5), 703–719.

Curtis, D. E., & Resnik, J. (1987). Images of justice. *The Yale Law Journal, 96*, 1727–1772.

Dorfman, L., & Schiraldi, V. (2001). Off balance: Youth, race & crime in the news. *Building Blocks for Youth.* Retrieved from http://www.cclp.org/documents/BBY/offbalance.pdf

Federal Advisory Committee on Juvenile Justice (FACJJ). (2006). *Annual report 2006.* Washington DC: Office of Juvenile Justice and Delinquency Prevention. Retrieved from http://www.ncjrs.gov/pdffiles1/ojjdp/218367.pdf

Federal Advisory Committee on Juvenile Justice (FACJJ). (2008). *Annual report 2008.* Washington DC: Office of Juvenile Justice and Delinquency Prevention. Retrieved from http://www.facjj.org/annualreports/ed_08-FACJJ%20Annual%20Report%2008.pdf

Federal Bureau of Investigation. (2008). *Crime in the United States: By community type, 2007.* Retrieved from http://www.fbi.gov/ucr/cius2007/data/table_02.html

Feld, B. C. (1995). The social context of juvenile justice administration: Racial disparities in an urban juvenile court. In K. Kempf Leonard, C. E. Pope, & W. H. Feyerherm (Eds.), *Minorities in juvenile justice* (pp. 66–97). Thousand Oaks, CA: Sage.

Guevara, L., Herz, D., & Spohn, C. (2006). Gender and juvenile justice decision making: What role does race play? *Feminist Criminology, 1*(4), 258–282.

Guevara, L., Herz, D., & Spohn, C. (2008). Race, gender, and legal counsel: Differential outcomes in two juvenile courts. *Youth Violence and Juvenile Justice, 6*(1), 83–104.

Hawkins, D. F., Laub, J. H., Lauritsen, J. L., & Cothern, L. (2000). Race, ethnicity, and serious and violent juvenile crime. *Juvenile Justice Bulletin.* Retrieved from http://www.ncjrs.org/pdffiles1/ojjdp/181202.pdf

Hawkins, D. F., & Leonard, K. K. (2005). *Our children, their children.* Chicago: University of Chicago Press.

Hsia, H. M., Bridges, G. S., & McHale, R. (2004). *Disproportionate minority confinement: 2002 update.* Washington DC: Office of Justice Programs. Retrieved from http://www.ncjrs.gov/pdffiles1/ojjdp/201240.pdf

Kempf Leonard, K., & Sontheimer, H. (1995). The role of race in juvenile justice in Pennsylvania. In K. Kempf Leonard, C. E. Pope, & W. H. Feyerherm (Eds.), *Minorities in juvenile justice* (pp. 98–127). Thousand Oaks, CA: Sage.

Next Steps for the Reader

- While access to juvenile court proceedings may be restricted, adult judicial proceedings are typically open to the public. Dedicate half a day to sit in a courtroom, watch the proceedings, and see how the different entities interact. Attempt to see cases where there is a private defense attorney and a public defender to compare the two. Can you see any differences between them?

- Spend time reflecting on what resources you would have at your disposal if you became a defendant in a judicial proceeding today. Do you know lawyers? Do you have money to pay for a defense? Would your job be safe pending the outcome of the trial? How could your life be affected if you did not have access to these resources, and if you could not be assured of keeping your job?

Additional Resources for Up-to-Date Facts and Stats

Burns Institute for Juvenile Justice Fairness & Equity
- Homepage—http://www.burnsinstitute.org/
- State Map—http://www.burnsinstitute.org/state_map.php

Juvenile Detention Alternatives Initiative
- JDAI Help Desk—http://www.jdaihelpdesk.org

Office of Juvenile Justice and Delinquency Prevention
- Homepage—http://www.ojjdp.gov/
- Easy Access to Juvenile Populations—http://www.ojjdp.gov/ojstatbb/ezapop/default.asp
- National Juvenile Court Data Archive—http://www.ojjdp.gov/ojstatbb/njcda/
- Statistical Briefing Book—http://www.ojjdp.gov/ojstatbb/default.asp

National Center for Juvenile Justice
- Homepage—http://www.ncjj.org/

National Council on Crime and Delinquency
- Homepage—http://www.nccd-crc.org/

National Criminal Justice Reference Service
- Juvenile Justice—http://www.ncjrs.gov/App/Topics/Topic.aspx?Topicid=122
- Gender/Race/Ethnicity—http://www.ncjrs.gov/App/Topics/Topic.aspx?topicid=137

Urban Institute
- Juvenile Justice and Youth Intervention—http://www.urban.org/justice/juvjustice.cfm

Kupchik, A. (2006). *Judging juveniles: Prosecuting adolescents in adult and juvenile courts*. New York: New York University Press.

Leiber, M. J. (2003). *The contexts of juvenile justice decision making: When race matters*. New York: State University of New York Press.

Leiber, M. J., & Fox, K. C. (2005). Race and the impact of detention on juvenile justice decision making. *Crime & Delinquency, 51*(4), 470–497.

Mastrofski, S. D., Worden, R. E., & Snipes, J. B. (1995). Law enforcement in a time of community policing. *Criminology, 33*(4), 539–559.

McCord, J., Spatz Widom, C., & Crowell, N. A. (Eds.). (2001). *Juvenile crime, juvenile justice*. Washington DC: National Academy Press.

McNulty, T. L., & Bellair, P. E. (2003). Explaining racial and ethnic differences in adolescent violence: Structural disadvantage, family well-being, and social capital. *Justice Quarterly, 20*(1), 1–31.

mikeoart.com. (2011). *Lady Justice* [drawing]. Personal drawing used with permission.

National Highway Traffic Safety Administration. (2008).
*2007 traffic safety annual assessment: Alcohol-impaired
driving fatalities.* Retrieved from http://www.nrd
.nhtsa.dot.gov/Pubs/811016.PDF

Piquero, A. R. (2008). Disproportionate minority contact.
The Future of Children, 18(2), 59–79.

Poe-Yamagata, E., & Jones, M. A. (2005). The juvenile justice system must stop discriminating against minority
youth. In A. C. Nakaya (Ed.), *Juvenile crime: Opposing viewpoints* (pp. 156–163). Farmington Hills, MI:
Greenhaven.

Poupart, L. M. (1995). Juvenile justice processing of Amer-
ican Indian youths: Disparity in one rural county. In
K. Kempf Leonard, C. E. Pope, & W. H. Feyerherm
(Eds.), *Minorities in juvenile justice* (pp. 179–200).
Thousand Oaks, CA: Sage.

Puzzanchera, C. (2009). Juvenile arrests 2007. *Juvenile Justice
Bulletin,* 1–12. Retrieved from http://www.ncjrs.gov/
pdffiles1/ojjdp/225344.pdf

Sealock, M. D., & Simpson, S. S. (1998). Unraveling bias
in arrest decisions: The role of juvenile offender type-
scripts. *Justice Quarterly, 15*(3), 427–457.

Shaffer, J. N., & Ruback, R. B. (2002). Violent victim-
ization as risk factor for violent offending among
juveniles. *Juvenile Justice Bulletin.* Retrieved from
http://www.ncjrs.gov/pdffiles1/ojjdp/195737.pdf

Sickmund, M. (2004). *Juveniles in corrections.* Washington
DC: Office of Juvenile Justice and Delinquency Prevention. Retrieved from http://www.ncjrs.gov/pdf-
files1/ojjdp/202885.pdf

Simons, R. L., Chen, Y. F., Stewart, E. A., & Brody, G. H.
(2003). Incidents of discrimination and risk for
delinquency: A longitudinal test of strain theory with
an African American sample. *Justice Quarterly, 20*(4),
827–854.

Singer, S. I. (1996). *Recriminalizing delinquency: Violent
juvenile crime and juvenile justice reform.* New York:
Cambridge University Press.

Snyder, H. N., & Sickmund, M. (2006). *Juvenile offenders
and victims: 2006 national report.* Pittsburgh, PA: National Center for Juvenile Justice.

Wordes, M., Bynum, T. S., & Corley, C. J. (1994). Locking
up youth: The impact of race on detention decisions.
Journal of Research in Crime and Delinquency, 31(2),
149–165.

5

Back of the School Bus
K–12 Education

PRIMARY AND SECONDARY EDUCATION ARE PEREN-nial topics of debate and discord throughout the United States. There is a host of research and literature detailing disparities in the education system and in access to educational opportunities. This chapter covers this multifaceted subject, beginning with the racial academic achievement gap. The merit of schools' heavy reliance on standardized testing is often the subject of heavy debate, but one cannot deny that standardized test results provide strong evidence that discrimination exists in our schools. Understanding why there is such a gap in performance between Black and White students is crucial, because "our efforts to eradicate the achievement gap will probably not be successful until we understand the precise mechanisms producing and reproducing the gap" (Van Laar & Sidanius, 2001, p. 236). As this chapter examines the achievement gap, and the factors that create and perpetuate it, attention is paid to a number of topics, including teacher/student mobility, classroom size and school funding, school discipline, and special education.

There are two caveats that are crucial philosophical underpinnings to the exploration of this topic. First, all children can learn. Second, there is no intellectual difference based on race. Therefore, if racial groups are under- or overperforming, the difference reflects discriminatory practices in our educational system, not inferiority of children. As such, the demographics of the United States' 73.9 million children found in Fig-ure 5.1 are an important baseline to highlight (Child Stats.gov, 2009).

If all children can learn, and if all racial groups are born with the same range of intellectual aptitude, then the achievement levels at any stage, on any scale, should roughly mirror Figure 5.1. However, as I describe in detail, they do not.

THE ACHIEVEMENT GAP

The achievement gap refers to the long-standing gulf between the academic success White students have experienced and the lower performance of students of color (Holcomb-McCoy, 2007). These gaps "are wide and persistent, well known and widely acknowledged. They arrive early and stay late—beginning before birth and continuing through high school" (Barton & Coley, 2009, p. 5). The achievement gap was initially used to measure educational attainment but has "shifted steadily from being an indicator of educational inequality to being a direct cause of socioeconomic inequality" (Harris & Herrington, 2006, p. 210).

Given the battery of tests our children take each year, the educational achievement gap is clear. Decade after decade, we have seen children of color lag behind White students on every conceivable educational measure. Although in the 1980s this gap decreased, such improvements were short-lived (Harris & Herrington,

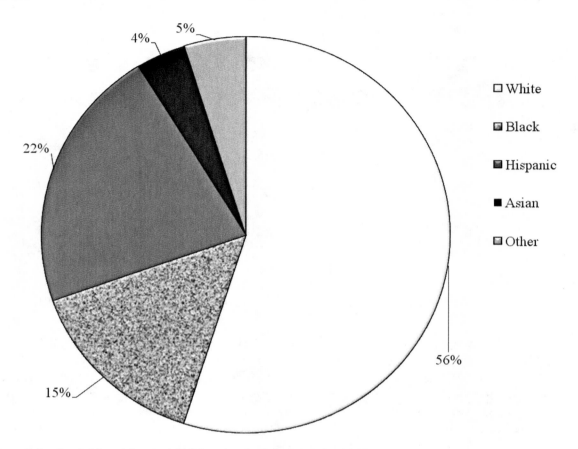

Figure 5.1   Racial Breakdown of Children in the United States, 2008

(ChildStats.gov, 2009)

2006; Johnston & Viadero, 2000; Kober, 2001; Lee, 2002). Research has further noted that "the black and white achievement gap was actually cut by . . . 33 percent in mathematics between 1970 and 1990, [but] it has been widening each year since" (Manning & Kovach, 2003, p. 25). Another example, detailed in Figure 5.2, is the test score gap between Black and White 13-year-olds in reading on a nationally standardized exam. The data depict the number of points by which Black children were behind White children.

The easiest way to describe the achievement gap is through testing measures akin to those represented in Figure 5.2. However, testing is far from a perfect measuring tool. Some scholars argue that testing is just another tool of the hierarchy to disenfranchise the poor and people of color. For example, the federal statute No Child Left Behind (NCLB) intended to increase school and teacher accountability while also raising

educational achievement. In reality, it has done quite the opposite; the test has instituted another barrier to success (Giroux & Schmidt, 2004; Kober, 2001). One article states further, "Standardized testing equates educational outcomes as a measurement of merit that diminishes the effect of systemic discrimination" (Hunter & Bartee, 2003, p. 153). We are left to believe that standardized testing measures a student's ability when, in reality, all it measures is what a child has experienced within the education system.

Such a focus on testing hurts all students because we squeeze out all of their creativity and individual talents. Instead, we hone their skills in sharpening #2 pencils and filling in ovals (Giroux & Schmidt, 2004). Even so, it is impossible to investigate the achievement gap without using the measures that define this gap. Therefore, much of this chapter uses data sets that are problematic from their inception, but are the best we have.

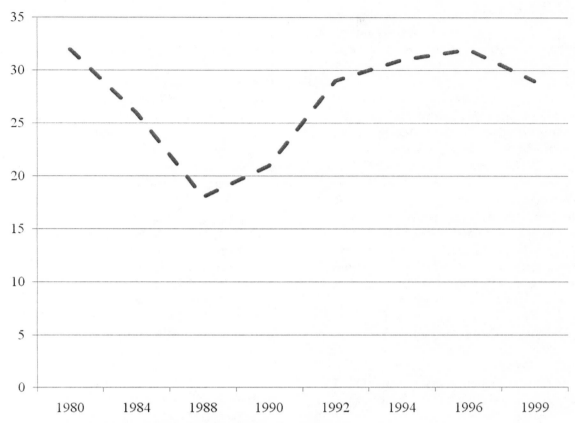

Figure 5.2 Black/White Average Reading Score Gap for 13-Year-Olds

(Kober, 2001)

This chapter first covers assessment data, focusing on two academic areas: reading and mathematics. While the choice to cover just two subjects withholds other viable data, the information presented will sufficiently detail the achievement gap.

There is one important stipulation. Some of the raw data will show that Asian/Pacific Islanders often perform on par with Whites. Failing to examine the multitude of overlapping factors behind this phenomenon only furthers the myth of Asians as the model minority. We must not perpetuate the lie that this group has somehow transcended race, worked hard, and prospered. The data presented are nationalized averages that withhold individual community differences. Places around the country, especially on the West Coast, parse out their data pertaining to Asian/Pacific Islander communities. In San Francisco, the school system uses nine demographic categories under the umbrella of the Asian/Pacific Islander data

set, and Seattle uses 16 different categories. This is crucial to note because individual Asian communities have been affected by achievement gaps for generations; however, the model minority myth has kept these facts hidden (Johnston, 2000).

The primary assessment this chapter uses is the National Assessment of Educational Progress (NAEP), the most widely used assessment to plot the educational progress of students. Called the nation's report card, the NAEP has collected data on schoolchildren's proficiency in math, reading, U.S. history, science, and many other topics for decades. Testing occurs in fourth, eighth, and twelfth grades, and, since there is a standardized method for exam administration at every level, the results provide easily comparable data. The results of each test can be broken down by subject area (i.e., math, reading), for individual populations (i.e., Black students) and for each state in the union (NAEP, 2009).

For each academic area the NAEP measures, there is a different method of scoring. However, one constant in these measurements is the division of achievement into three levels: Basic, Proficient, and Advanced.

- *Basic*—denoting partial mastery of prerequisite knowledge and skills that are fundamental for proficient work at each grade assessed.
- *Proficient*—representing solid academic performance for each grade assessed. Students reaching this level have demonstrated competency over challenging subject matter, including subject-matter knowledge, application of such knowledge to real-world situations, and analytical skills appropriate to the subject matter.
- *Advanced*—denoting superior performance at each grade assessed. (NAEP, n.d.)

For each subject area covered in this chapter, I report these achievement levels alongside the nationwide data set. The comparison of national scores against the achievement level data is an important reference point in several instances. For example, I present data stipulating that students of color are "X" number of points behind White students on a measure. In this fictitious example, that gap of X points is important, and closing it is essential to furthering educational opportunities for all students. If White students are only testing at the Basic level on an assessment, the fact that students of color lag behind is concerning. But our goal is not to get the students of color to perform at the same level as White children. Instead, we should seek to erase this gap while also increasing the educational attainment of all students beyond mere Basic levels (Singham, 2003).

This is an important reminder that we cannot cast White students' scores as the desired achievement level. Even though that group may be on top, this does not denote a ceiling on accomplishment.

Reading

Reading is, perhaps, the most fundamental skill for academic success. Many take this skill for granted, but reading is not a naturally occurring ability. We only learn and improve through intentional instruction and practice. Unfortunately, not all communities have the same resources for developing this ability.

Much research has detailed the growing gulf between low-income and high-income elementary students as it relates to reading achievement. This separation is present when the children enroll in kindergarten, as detailed in Table 5.1 (Neuman, 2005).

It is clear from these results that high-SES children are more than twice as likely as low-SES children to be able to distinguish letters in the alphabet and more than five times likely to identify beginning sounds of words. These children are also more likely to be able to write their name and can use 32 million more words than their low-SES peers (Neuman, 2005). This often starts a cycle in which low-SES children feel like incompetent readers, making them less inclined to want to read, thereby exacerbating their poor reading abilities (Allington & McGill-Franzen, 2003). In addition, while research clearly delineates an effect by SES, data from the NAEP detail a racial disparity.

The NAEP for Reading was last administered in 2007, and the achievement levels for Basic, Proficient, and Advanced were set as shown in Table 5.2.

Table 5.3 gives the 2007 scores on this Reading assessment and, as a point of comparison, the scores dating back to 1998.

Two facts are readily apparent from these raw scores. First, in 2007, no racial group is performing at or above the Proficient achievement level. White and Asian/Pacific Islander children are close but not quite there. Second, these raw scores clearly depict a disparity in reading scores as the Black, Hispanic, and Native American/Alaskan Native students were all below their White classmates. Figure 5.3 highlights this disparity

TABLE 5.1			
Reading Achievement Gap Indicators by SES, Kindergarten (Neuman, 2005)			
	Low-SES Children	*High-SES Children*	*Gap (Low–High)*
Distinguish Letters	39%	85%	−46%
Recognize Word Sounds	10%	51%	−41%
Write Their Name	54%	76%	−22%
Total Word Experience	13 Million Words	45 Million Words	−32 Million Words

TABLE 5.2				
Fourth-Grade Reading Achievement Level Cutoff Scores (NAEP, 2005)				
	Scoring	*Basic*	*Proficient*	*Advanced*
Reading	0–500	208	238	268

TABLE 5.3					
NAEP Fourth-Grade Average Reading Scores (National Center for Education Statistics [NCES], 2007)					
	Reading *NAEP Average Scores—4th Grade*				
	White	*Black*	*Hispanic*	*Asian/Pacific Islander*	*Native American/ Alaskan Native*
2007	231	203	205	232	203
2005	229	200	203	229	204
2003	229	198	200	226	202
2002	229	199	201	224	207
2000	224	190	190	225	214
1998	225	193	193	215	No data

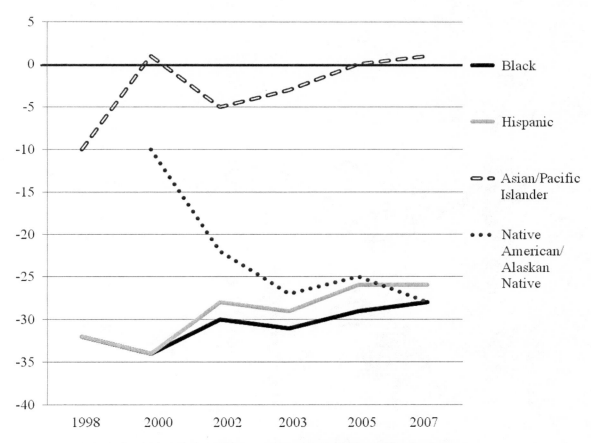

Figure 5.3   NAEP Fourth-Grade Reading Achievement Gap Compared to White Students

(NCES, 2007)

further by delineating the varying reading achievement gaps.

The report from the National Center for Education Statistics (NCES, 2007) touts a closing of the reading achievement gap; however, this is too grand an extrapolation from this data set. From 1998 to 2007, the Black disparity decreased 4 points and the Hispanic 6 points; from 2002 to 2007, the Native American/Alaskan Native disparity grew by 6 points. Such results are far from perfect and actually hide another facet to these data. Figure 5.4 exemplifies how the racial groups comprise the achievement levels delineated in the NAEP.

These scores are not presented in the prominently displayed report published by NAEP. These data are freely available to the public, but one must dig to find the stories these assessment scores tell. The NAEP reports a closing of the achievement gap, but we can see that such nationally averaged numbers can hide a different facet of disparity. Over half of White students, 57%, score at the Basic level or below. This is a number no one should be proud of, and it is of vital na-

tional interest that it be raised. And yet, when the data for Black, Hispanic, and Native American/Alaskan Native children at the Basic level or below are computed, that statistic exceeds 80% in each group. For Black children alone, the statistic is 86% at or below Basic (NCES, n.d.).

Closing the achievement gap does not mean raising children of color's scores to the level of Whites'. As seen, White children's scores are not something to be proud of in the United States. However, even when adding the statistics together from the Advanced achievement level for Black, Hispanic, and Native American/Alaskan Native groups (9%), their combined scores still trail their White counterparts (11%). More work is required on multiple fronts.

Math

Albert Einstein once said, "Do not worry about your difficulties in mathematics; I assure you that mine are greater" (as quoted in Dowker, 2005, p. 15). If only Einstein's humble math abilities could be channeled into our children today to eliminate the many distress-

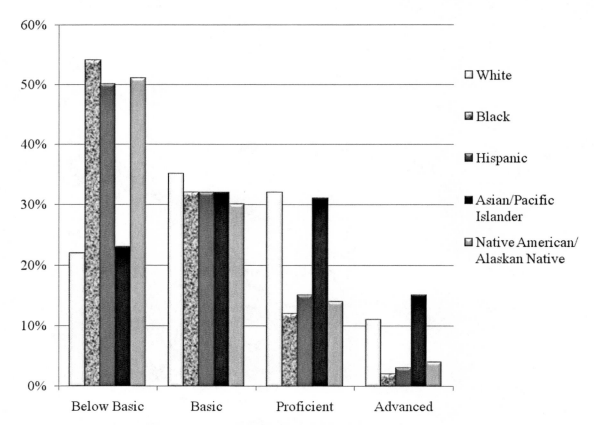

Figure 5.4   NAEP Fourth-Grade Reading Scores by Achievement Level, 2007 Data

(NCES, n.d.)

ing statistics that detail how SES and race directly affect one's mathematics education.

Regarding the influence of SES, one researcher noted, "wealth, particularly a family's income-producing financial assets, such as stocks and bonds, was a powerful predictor of math achievement" (Sacks, 2007, p. 17). Wealth can affect the types of educational tools and resources children have at their disposal. However, SES is not all about one's bank account; higher SES also allows children to garner greater knowledge and skills that will positively influence their education. For example, research supports that children of lower SES have parents who are less involved in their schooling, compared to those of higher SES (Sheldon & Epstein, 2005; Simon, 2008). Such lack of involvement can stem from parents feeling intimidated by the academic environment or believing that no matter what effort they put forth, the school will disregard them. This affects children's expectations of their performance on a math exam, thereby exacerbating an already troublesome problem (Lee & Bowen, 2006). The accumulated effects of this reality are prominent in the percentage breakdown of high school seniors who excel at math, illustrated in Table 5.4.

Concomitantly, in exploring the relationship between race and math achievement, scores show that White children widely outpace Hispanic children. In examining this phenomenon, researchers have investigated how academic outcomes are influenced by related factors such as child self-efficacy, which is the level of competence a child believes he or she possesses; amount of praise the child receives; how many experiences the child had where he or she mastered an element of mathematics; and their reported anxiety concerning math. These data are reported in Table 5.5, and all racial differences are statistically significant ($p < .05$) (Stevens, Olivarez, & Hamman, 2006).

These data were collected in West and South Texas with 666 children ranging from 8 to 18 years old. The test for math performance was a standardized exam, called the Woodcock-Johnson III Tests of Achievement. Using this exam allowed researchers to make performance comparisons for different grade levels using a reliable and valid testing instrument. The researchers collected math self-efficacy data by giving students a variety of grade-appropriate math problems and asking them to rate their confidence in their ability to solve the equation on a seven-point linear scale. Last, the Mathematics Experiences Scale (MES) collected the data on praise received, mastery experiences,

TABLE 5.4 High School Seniors Scoring in Top Quartile in Math (Sacks, 2007)	
	High School Seniors Scoring in Top Quartile in Math
Low SES	6.5%
Middle SES	23.0%
High SES	50.0%

TABLE 5.5 Children's Underlying Factors Affecting Math Scores (Stevens et al., 2006)		
	Hispanic Students	*White Students*
Math Performance	101.90	105.82
Math Self-Efficacy	97.27	102.15
Praise Received	10.14	10.78
Mastery Occurrences	9.95	10.63
Anxiety Present	10.97	12.03

and math anxiety. The authors created the MES for this research to measure these variables. It is important to note that the lower scores on the Anxiety scale in Table 5.5 denote higher anxiety (Stevens et al., 2006).

Table 5.5 depicts statistically significant differences favoring White students on every measure. The researchers wrote, "Hispanic students are typically at a disadvantage, experiencing significantly lower mathematics performance, feelings of self-efficacy, amounts of praise, and levels of mastery, as well as higher levels of mathematics anxiety" (Stevens et al., 2006, p. 171).

Whether it is race or class, or the combined effects of both, these data relating the variables that can affect math performance set the stage for the NAEP data. In this instance we explore the mathematics scores for eighth graders from 1996 to 2009. Table 5.6 describes the achievement levels set for the NAEP.

This baseline of performance expectations sets the stage for the NAEP assessment data from 1996 through 2009 for eighth-grade mathematics in Table 5.7.

Referencing the NAEP achievement levels in Table 5.6, all groups except one, Asian/Pacific Islanders, have average scores below the Proficient achievement level in 2009. Additionally, we can again document the achievement gap between Black, Hispanic, and Native American/Alaskan Native students and their White counterparts. Figure 5.5 plots this mathematic achievement gap over time.

TABLE 5.6				
Eighth-Grade Mathematics Achievement Level Cutoff Scores (NAEP, 2006)				
	Scoring	*Basic*	*Proficient*	*Advanced*
Mathematics	0–500	262	299	333

TABLE 5.7					
NAEP Eighth-Grade Average Mathematics Scores (NCES, 2009)					
Mathematics *NAEP Average Scores—8th Grade*					
	White	*Black*	*Hispanic*	*Asian/Pacific Islander*	*Native American/ Alaskan Native*
2009	293	261	266	301	266
2007	291	260	265	297	264
2005	289	255	262	295	264
2003	288	252	259	291	263
2000	284	244	253	288	259
1996	281	240	251	No data	No data

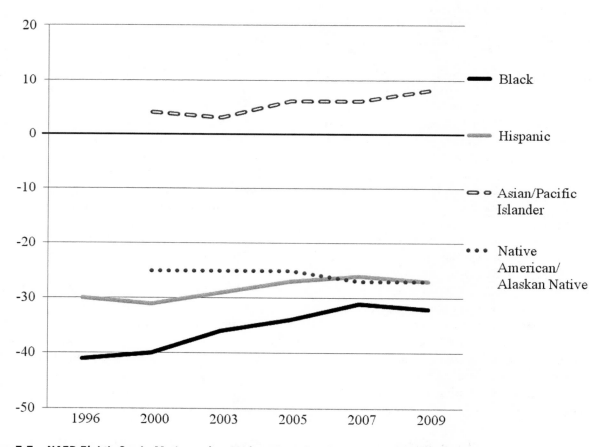

Figure 5.5   NAEP Eighth-Grade Mathematics Achievement Gap Compared to White Students

(NCES, 2009)

The disparity between Blacks and Whites has diminished in the last 13 years by nine points; we cannot say the same for other communities, however. In the same amount of time, we only see a three- and two-point diminishment in this gap for Hispanics and Native American/Alaskan Natives, respectively. Yet, while this gap is unjust, we must view these scores through the lens of the NAEP achievement levels. The NAEP again did not report these data in the final publication of these results.

The percentages from Figure 5.6 of students at or below the Basic level for mathematics are White, 57%; Black, 87%; Hispanic, 83%; Asian/Pacific Islander, 46%; and American Indian, 82%. Once again, our desire is not to simply raise children of color's scores to be the same as White students. Much more work needs to be done across all communities of children.

UNDERLYING ACHIEVEMENT GAP FACTORS

There are a variety of interrelated factors that create and perpetuate this achievement gap including:

teacher/student mobility, classroom size and school funding, school discipline, and special education. While this section covers each topic separately, it is vital to remember such entities overlap and interact with one another.

Teacher/Student Mobility

Several factors influence the classroom experience and the teacher is the most central. There is a wealth of research on teacher expectations as they pertain to race. Many researchers have contended that "African Americans and Latinos [are] the targets of negative stereotypes about intellectual ability while European Americans and Asian Americans are the beneficiaries of neutral or positive stereotypes about intellectual ability" (McKown & Weinstein, 2008, pp. 236–237). In a wide-scale analysis of 39 data sets examining the link between teachers' expectations and students' race, researchers found "small but meaningful correlations" between these factors (Tenenbaum & Ruck, 2007, p. 261). In each instance, teachers tended to have higher expectations for their White students

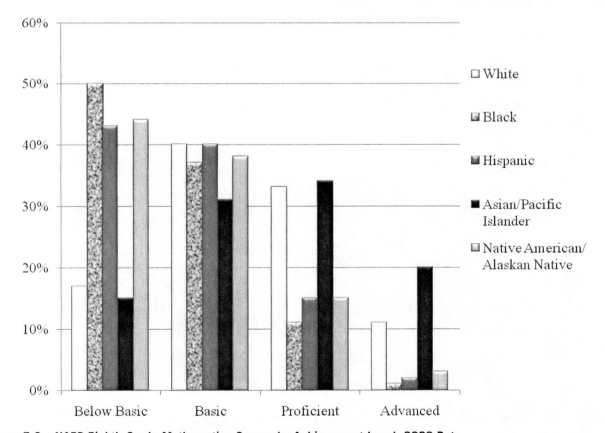

Figure 5.6   NAEP Eighth-Grade Mathematics Scores by Achievement Level, 2009 Data

(NCES, n.d.)

than for their children of color. In addition to these intellectual expectations, teachers in the United States, who are predominantly White, may be more prone to misunderstand the behavior of students from other cultures (Norman, Ault, Bentz, & Meskimen, 2001). Teachers' biased expectations, when coupled with their failure to accurately interpret student behaviors or communications, lead students to achieve only at the level that is expected, regardless of their actual ability. This is otherwise known as the self-fulfilling prophecy (Cooper, 2010).

It may be impossible to determine definitively whether teacher expectations exist or the effect of those expectations on the educational outcomes of students of color. However, researchers have explored other factors involving teachers; the first is teacher continuity. White students tend to have the highest likelihood of having the same teacher throughout the academic year. Figure 5.7 contains data from 2000 that detail the percentage of fourth graders who retained the same teacher throughout the year.

As reported, 82% of White students have the benefit of continuous instruction from the same teacher throughout the year. For Black students, that percentage decreases by 25 percentage points. Similar results were found when examining eighth-grade children whose mathematics teacher departed before the end of the academic year. Figure 5.8 details these results.

This disparity between Black and White children stands at 24 percentage points. The disruption caused by a teacher leaving during the academic year can have disastrous effects on a child's education. Administrators must take time to recruit, hire, and train new teachers. This is a time-consuming task, taking administrators' attention away from other important issues at the school (Denson, 2004). Furthermore, research has detailed that teachers with the least amount of experience are hired into the positions with the highest turnover rate. These inexperienced teachers are often associated with students' lower academic performance (Clotfelter, Ladd, & Vigdor, 2005; Freeman, Scafidi, & Sjoquist, 2005).

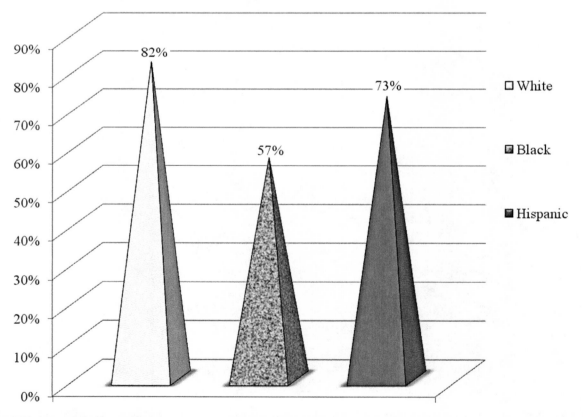

Figure 5.7   Fourth Graders Who Started and Ended the Year With the Same Teacher

(Barton, 2003)

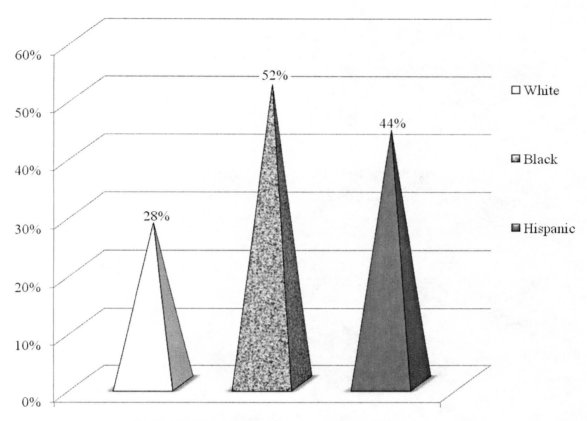

Figure 5.8   Eighth-Grade Math Teacher Departed Before End of School Year

(Barton & Coley, 2009)

Not only is teacher continuity at stake, school continuity is also an issue. The data in Figure 5.9 stem from the U.S. Census Bureau and show that Black students have a much higher propensity to change schools during the academic year.

This inconsistency in a child's education carries "lower achievement levels and slower academic pacing" when compared to the education of stable children (Hartman & Leff, 2006, p. 270). Many factors can bring about conditions that necessitate school changes. Examples include parental job opportunities, affordable housing, homelessness, and transportation issues, all of which are more likely to be the plight of the poor and people of color (Crowley, 2003; Julianelle & Foscarinis, 2003; Rumberger, 2003).

Classroom Size and School Funding

It is common knowledge that small class sizes are advantageous to both students and teachers. The following excerpt captures this sentiment well:

From the perspective of the teacher, smaller classes are obviously more convenient and easier to teach than larger ones. Fewer students permit teachers to devote more time to each student, spend less time grading exams and have greater control over the classes. Smaller classes may also decrease disciplinary problems and provide more time for personal involvement with students. (Ansalone, 2009, p. 120)

However, as seen in Table 5.8, there is a positive correlation between the size of a school's student of color population and the number of students in each class. As the percentage of students of color rises, so, too, does the percentage of classrooms that have 25 or more students.

In his book, *The Shame of a Nation: The Restoration of Apartheid Schooling in America*, Jonathan Kozol (2005) compiles many stories of obscenely overcrowded classrooms throughout the United States.

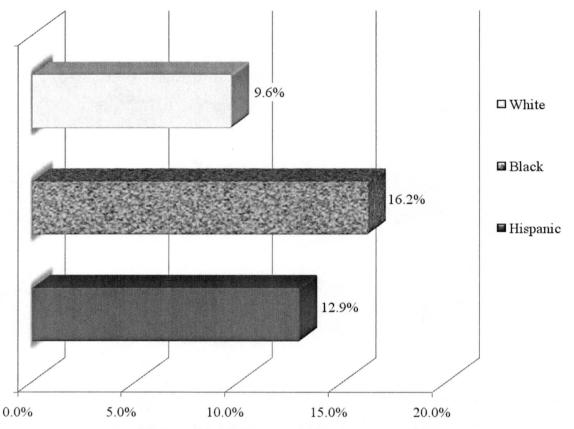

Figure 5.9　Six- to 17-Year-Old Children Who Changed Schools in the Previous Year

(Barton & Coley, 2009)

Fremont High School in Los Angeles enrolls 5,000 predominantly Hispanic students and has fewer than 220 classes, resulting in 33 to more than 40 students per class. Another school, located in the Bronx and serving primarily Black and Latino students, has class sizes of 34 or more, and the school's four kindergartens and one sixth-grade class all share the same space. However, when a public school in more affluent Greenwich Village in Manhattan expected a fourth-grade class to swell from 26 to 32 students, the parents united to raise the money privately to fund hiring another teacher.

Many are quick to argue that money is not the answer to all problems. While this may be true, those most likely to invoke such an argument are often those with the money. Such arguments are an attempt to gloss over the rampant disparity in school funding. Kozol (2005) details the funding per pupil of nine schools as well as describing their racial composition, detailed in Table 5.9.

The disparity could not be clearer. Moreover, we all know what school we would choose for our own children if the only information available were funding per pupil.

School Discipline

Much like juveniles in the justice system, covered in chapter 4, when we discuss school discipline, many forget we are talking about children. Some forget that those who act out at school "have minimal capacities for non-self-interested deliberation, and even less to

TABLE 5.8		
Teachers With 25 or More Students per Class		
(Barton & Coley, 2009)		
	Teachers With 25 or More Students per Class (2004 data)	
Below 15% Children of Color	14%	
15%–49% Children of Color	17%	
Over 50% Children of Color	23%	

TABLE 5.9
Spending per Student, 2002–2003 Academic Year (Kozol, 2005)

	Per Student Spending	Percent of Students Black or Hispanic
Chicago, IL, Area Schools		
New Trier High School	$14,909	2%
Lake Forest High School	$14,563	1%
Chicago Public Schools; K–12	$8,482	87%
Philadelphia, PA, Area Schools		
Lower Merion; K–12	$17,261	9%
Philadelphia Public Schools; K–12	$9,299	79%
Detroit, MI, Area Schools		
Bloomfield Hills; K–12	$12,825	8%
Detroit Public Schools; K–12	$9,576	95%
Milwaukee, WI, Area Schools		
Nicolet High School	$13,698	21%
Milwaukee Public Schools; K–12	$10,874	77%

join rational conclusions with actions. They are impulsive, erratic, irrational, egocentric and easily influenced. They make mistakes because they are young, not bad" (Goodman, 2006, p. 226). We often ascribe adult levels of responsible choice making and personal responsibility to those who are not developmentally able to bear such accountability.

Instead, we must relocate our focus from problematizing the child to focusing on the system dispensing judgment (Monroe, 2005). Morris argues, "schools tend to reproduce and even exaggerate inequalities of race, class, and gender" (2005, p. 26). These inequalities stem from the homogeneous teachers and administrators setting "norms" for the school and assigning sanctions when these "norms" are violated. When teachers administer sanctions, a child can be labeled as a "problem," causing disastrous consequences on that child's educational achievement and future opportunities.

Some scholars have argued that such labeling can enact a school-to-prison pipeline whereby a child's life is set on track toward the Department of Corrections from an early age (Fenning & Rose, 2007). Additionally, the discipline a child receives at school "has been linked with posttraumatic stress disorder (PTSD), depression, anxiety, aggressive behavior in and out of school, academic failure, and school dropout" (Cameron & Sheppard, 2006, p. 15). Such phenomena have devastating consequences and are experienced disproportionately by children of color throughout the United States.

Research has long purported a discipline gap in the U.S. school system linked to the achievement gap. This decades old reality is still supported by the contemporary data. To begin, the U.S. Department of Education releases statistical projections for the entire country on our education system. Part of these projections relate to student discipline and are detailed in Table 5.10.

TABLE 5.10
2006 School Discipline Projections From the U.S. Department of Education
(U.S. Department of Education, 2006)

	Total School Population	Corporal Punishment	Suspension	Expulsion
White	56.42%	53.47%	39.13%	37.25%
Black	17.13%	35.67%	37.40%	37.86%
Hispanic	20.41%	8.34%	20.15%	21.69%

An important note is that the statistics on corporal punishment are from states where such discipline is legal. As can be seen, Whites are not subject to corporal punishment, suspension, or expulsion at rates comparable to their percentage of the population. The data on Hispanics reflect conflict in the research, where some results purport disproportional discipline, but others debunk that argument (Skiba, Michael, Nardo, & Peterson, 2002). However, the Black population is about twice as likely to receive any of the three across the board. The contemporary research supports this claim in U.S. schools.

The most severe discipline a child can receive, in my opinion, is corporal punishment. We can quantify suspension and expulsion by how many days a student was absent. However, we cannot quantify how hard a child was hit and what psychological effect it had on that child. As of the 2006–2007 school year, 30 states plus the District of Columbia prohibited corporal punishment in school. This still leaves 20 states where it is legally permissible for a teacher to strike a child in the pursuit of learning (Center for Effective Discipline [CED], n.d.). As of November 2009, 109 countries around the world have forbidden the use of such discipline in school. Some may find it interesting that countries on this list include Afghanistan, Iran, Iraq, Libya, and Venezuela (Global Initiative to End All Corporal Punishment of Children, 2009).

However, back in the United States, "African-American students comprise 17% of all public school students in the U.S., but are 36% of those who have corporal punishment inflicted on them, more than twice the rate of white students" (CED, n.d.). Additionally, research has found that when race and class are correlated together, Black children with low SES were disproportionately the recipients of corporal punishment ($p < .05$) (Owen, 2005). Furthermore, hitting often leads to unintentional side effects. "The modeling of punitive discipline may unintentionally suggest to students that the use of aggressive and coercive action is appropriate" (Cameron & Sheppard, 2006, p. 18).

Beyond physical discipline, research related to teacher referrals for discipline, suspensions, and expulsions all supports the U.S. Department of Education's projected statistics. One study, detailed in Figure 5.10, from a large middle school district in the Midwest, found a sizeable statistical gap between White and Black students.

These gaps are all statistically significant ($p < .01$). Black students represent nearly 81% of all expulsions, an overrepresentation of nearly 25%, while the same statistic is 17% for White students, underrepresented at the same margin, 25% (Skiba et al., 2002).

In another study, researchers reported racial differences in the causes for student discipline referral. For White students, the most often cited reasons were "smoking, leaving without permission, vandalism, and obscene language," and for the Black students it was "disrespect, excessive noise, threat, and loitering" (Skiba et al., 2002, p. 332). While it is difficult to derive the severity in outcome from each of these referrals, there is one notable aspect. The referrals for White students stemmed from quantifiable behaviors, and the referrals for Black students stemmed from behaviors where the administrator had to make some level of inference regarding behavior severity. Any person can point out smoking or obscene language without the need of training. However, determining disrespect and *excessive* noise is something conducted through the lens of the administrator. This is an area in need of development if we want to diminish unequal treatment based on race (Skiba et al., 2002).

Another study sought to delve deeper into the subjectivity of teachers and administrators in student discipline. First, the authors found a similar racial disproportion in student discipline, specifically as it related to referrals for defiance, as reported in Table 5.11.

In comparing the total number of students referred for defiance against their relative proportion in the whole school population, Black students were significantly more likely ($p < .001$) to receive a referral. Yet, how exactly does one determine that a student is defiant? This is a very difficult question to answer. The researchers investigated further to seek possible differences between teachers that might explain these results. For the teachers who referred students for defiance compared to teachers who did not, there was a statistically significant difference in perception of student engagement in education ($p < .001$). These teachers are all talking about the same group of children. Nonetheless, some educators had labeled some children as defiant and, therefore, less academically engaged, while other teachers found no issue with the same students and determined they were adequately engaged in classroom study (Gregory & Weinstein, 2008).

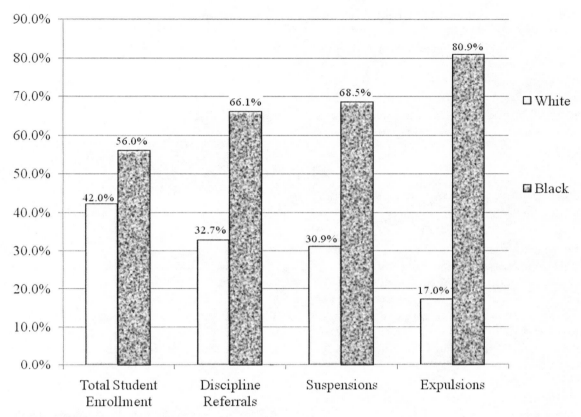

Figure 5.10   Student Discipline by Race

(Skiba et al., 2002)

When surveying the student body, the children corroborated these results. They related that their behavior and treatment varied greatly depending upon the teacher. Certain teachers earned the trust of students, which significantly correlated ($p < .01$) with the teacher's belief in the academic potential of the students and the degree to which the students believed their teacher cared about them (Gregory & Weinstein, 2008) (see Table 5.12).

Such data raise "questions about whether defiance in school among African American students is a situational and interactional phenomenon between teachers and students" as opposed to an objective, quantifiable act requiring sanction (Gregory & Weinstein, 2008, p. 469). After all, in this specific study, 86% of discipline referrals for defiance came from only one to three adults in the school. This is a low number of educators enforcing norms and affecting the experience of many students. Other research has

TABLE 5.11
Race Comparisons in Discipline Referrals for Defiance (Gregory & Weinstein, 2008)

	Total School Population	Total Discipline Referral for Defiance
White	37%	5%
Black	30%	58%

TABLE 5.12
Student/Teacher Perception Correlations (Gregory & Weinstein, 2008)

	Student Trust of Teacher
Teacher Believes Students Have High Academic Potential	.58
Teacher High Care	.88

purported that "Schools in which students report that the rules are fair and the discipline is consistently managed experience less disorder, regardless of the type of school and community" (Gottfredson, Gottfredson, Payne, & Gottfredson, 2005, p. 435). However, for other educators, whether consciously or unconsciously, "the 'blackness' of students seem[s] to indicate aggression and forcefulness" requiring their corrective action (Morris, 2005, p. 44).

Special Education

Educational administrators disproportionately refer children of color for special education services. It is important to state that this difference between races, much like the divergence in school discipline, is a function of the school system's biased norms. "Educators tend to see Whiteness as the norm and consequently the academic skills, behavior, and social skills of African American and other students of color are constantly compared with those of their White peers" (Blanchett, 2006, p. 27). In such a system, if a student of color acts differently, that student has deviated from the White-norm, and is thereby more likely to be referred to special education. Being placed into special education can have a significant effect on the hopes and dreams of our children (O'Connor & DeLuca Fernandez, 2006).

Of course, as outlined in chapters 2 and 3, we know children of color are more likely to be poor, lack access to adequate health care, and live in polluted neighborhoods. Given this information, it may be tempting to blame these disproportionate special education referral rates on these factors. However, this allows "Disability [to] become a more socially accepted . . . category of marginalization for students of color" (Ferri & Connor, 2005a, p. 454). We cannot defer to those biological effects as being the only variable. Again, it is our society that sets rules for who fits in and who does not, who will achieve and who will not. These rules are embedded into the fabric of our lives (O'Connor & DeLuca Fernandez, 2006).

Special education is similar to school discipline in that there are objective aspects relating to a child requiring special education and subjective factors. For the objective factors, such as deafness and blindness, there is no racial overrepresentation (Ferri & Connor, 2005b). The racial discrimination is found on subjective measures where "diagnosis rests on the 'art' of professional judgment" (O'Connor & DeLuca Fernandez, 2006, p. 6).

To serve as a baseline of data, the National Health Interview Survey (NHIS) conducted by the Centers for Disease Control and Prevention (CDC) compiles statistics collected from parental disclosure relating to a host of disabilities. Table 5.13 outlines the racial breakdown for children and their rates of diagnosis for Learning Disability (LD).

TABLE 5.13 Learning Disability Diagnosis by Race: NHIS 1997–2001 (Pastor & Reuben, 2005)	
	Learning Disability Diagnosis
White	4.3%
Hispanic	4.8%
Black	5.6%

There is a statistically significant difference ($p = .05$) in reported rates of diagnosis, with Black students having a higher likelihood of being labeled as having an LD. Identical results, which appear in Table 5.14, are found when comparing SES, as derived from income level and LD diagnosis ($p < .001$).

TABLE 5.14 Learning Disability Diagnosis by SES: NHIS 1997–2001 (Pastor & Reuben, 2005)	
Poverty Limit	*Learning Disability Diagnosis*
400% >	3.3%
200–399%	4.1%
100–199%	5.9%
< 100%	7.5%

While the statistical differences among Tables 5.13 and 5.14 may not be great, when we spread these disparities out among an entire country of children, the gravity of the disparity is impossible to ignore.

On a smaller scale, researchers also found differential rates of diagnosis for mental retardation in Atlanta's metropolitan school district. Blacks were more than twice as likely as Whites to be diagnosed with mental retardation. Even in parsing this diagnosis down to those with mild to moderate and those with profound mental retardation, as done in Table 5.15, the same racial disparity is evident (Karapurkar Bhasin, Brocksen, Nonkin Avchen, & Van Naarden Braun, 2006).

These researchers cited this differential rate of diagnosis as possibly stemming from cultural problems with

TABLE 5.15 Mental Retardation Prevalence (per 1,000 Children) in Eight-Year-Olds (Karapurkar Bhasin et al., 2006)			
	Mental Retardation	*Mild to Moderate Mental Retardation*	*Profound Mental Retardation*
White	7.0	3.8	1.9
Black	16.9	10.9	4.8

the assessment as well as other SES variables. Other research also supports such assessment bias as it relates to diagnosis and special education (Harry & Klingner, 2005; Rhodes, Ochoa, & Ortiz, 2005).

Those with a learning disability or mental retardation are not the only ones served through special education; children deemed to have an emotional disturbance also use these services (Wagner, Kutash, Duchnowski, Epstein, & Sumi, 2005). Emotional disturbances can include anxiety, depression, or obsessive-compulsive disorder. Illustrated in Figure 5.11, research using two national assessments funded by the

U.S. Department of Education found the same racial overrepresentation in elementary and middle school Black and White students.

This statistically significant discrepancy between diagnosis and overall population representation follows students into high school, as reported in Figure 5.12.

These assessments also reported data exemplifying poverty as a statistically significant factor in the diagnosis of emotional disturbance. However, with the overlap between race and SES, it is a judicious speculation that the economic stress in poor households, which are also more likely to comprise people of color, is a

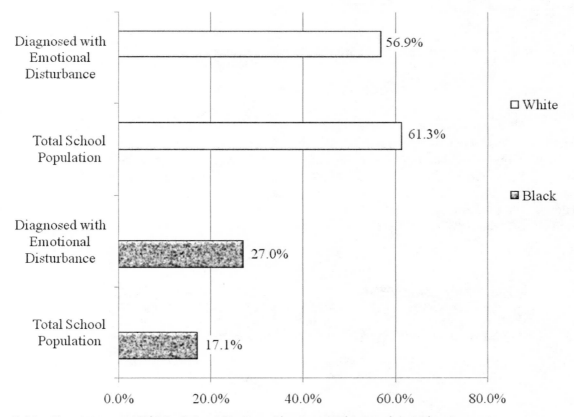

Figure 5.11 Elementary and Middle School Students Diagnosed With Emotional Disturbance

(Wagner et al., 2005)

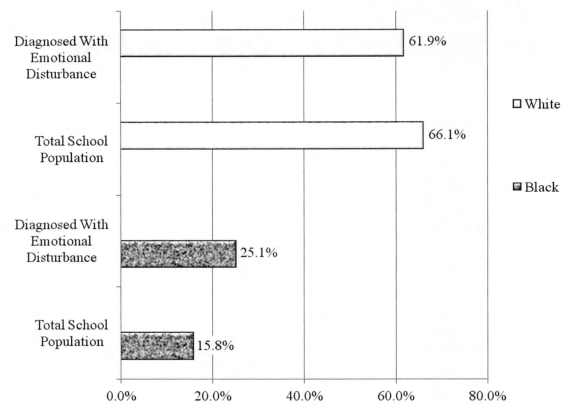

Figure 5.12   High School Students Diagnosed With Emotional Disturbance

(Wagner et al., 2005)

mitigating variable in the increased level of emotional disturbances seen in children (Wagner et al., 2005). Relating back to special education, other researchers took this idea further, stating, "in those cases where poverty makes any contribution to explaining disproportionality, its effect is primarily to magnify already existing racial disparities" (Skiba, Poloni-Staudinger, Simmons, Feggins-Azziz, & Chung, 2005, p. 141).

Nonetheless, even if we were to assume that all children with a diagnosis are in need of assistance, the assistance garnered is far from equitable. Table 5.16 exemplifies some interventions for children with basic action difficulties. A basic action difficulty includes issues a child may have in sensory reception, movement, cognitive action, and/or emotional or behavioral responses (Pastor, Reuben, & Loeb, 2009).

TABLE 5.16 Interventions for 5- to 17-Year-Old Children With Basic Actions Difficulty, Last 12 Months (Pastor et al., 2009)			
	White	*Black*	*Hispanic*
Medical Specialist	26.9%	16.4%	19.6%
Therapist	17.0%	15.2%	14.9%
Mental Health Professional	28.5%	23.5%	21.9%
Prescription in last 3 months	43.8%	32.7%	28.1%
At least 10 medical visits in last year	17.1%	9.6%	12.0%

Even if we assume an appropriate diagnosis, there is no guarantee treatment will be received. White children have the greatest odds of garnering the assistance outlined in Table 5.16. Furthermore, every racial difference in Table 5.16 is statistically significant ($p < .01$), except in the category for having seen a therapist.

Perhaps the best evidence of this gap in special education is the successes found in reducing disparity when new, culturally attuned educational tactics are used. One such example is Instructional Consultation (IC) teams. These teams work to "improve, enhance, and increase student achievement through improving, enhancing, and increasing teachers' performance" (Gravois & Rosenfield, 2006, p. 45). This instructional innovation is based on creating an interdisciplinary educational team of teachers, administrators, and support staff. These teams are highly collaborative in consulting on student needs and evaluate themselves critically in relation to student success. They support teachers at every level to better meet children's needs without simply referring problem students to special education. When an educator encounters an issue with a student, that teacher asks an IC team to help devise an appropriate response as opposed to taking sole responsibility for making crucial decisions concerning a student's life. As reported in Table 5.17, when these schools were compared to non–IC team-employing schools over a three-year span, the former had fewer special education referrals for students of color.

And, even beyond this decrease in referrals, there is a decrease in the number of students actually placed in special education, as evidenced in Table 5.18.

TABLE 5.17 Referral of Students of Color for Special Education Evaluation (Gravois & Rosenfield, 2006)			
	2002	*2003*	*2004*
IC Team School	3.3%	2.4%	1.9%
Baseline School	5.2%	3.9%	4.3%

TABLE 5.18 Placement of Students of Color for Special Education (Gravois & Rosenfield, 2006)			
	2002	*2003*	*2004*
IC Team School	1.9%	1.6%	1.2%
Baseline School	3.0%	2.0%	3.2%

In both cases, by the third year, the IC team school referred and placed far fewer students of color into special education (Gravois & Rosenfield, 2006).

Employing tactics such as IC teams represents a win for everybody. The teachers win because they receive support to teach all of their students. The students win because those who should remain in general education stay on target. For students who need special education assistance, they do not have classes full of students who should not be there soaking up resource time. And finally, the administration and community win because fewer resources need to be spent on expensive special education services. It is rare that we can solve a problem this complex in a manner benefiting all parties involved.

CONCLUSION

The achievement gap and other educational issues are not created solely in the schools. The classroom may perpetuate and support them, but these issues begin long before enrollment. Every chapter of this book adds to a story of how or why children of color are performing at lower levels, and none of the data point to inherent problems with children. The problem is embedded throughout society.

While we have to increase the attention we pay to educational disparity, we must frame such conversations appropriately. For instance, Gloria Ladson-Billings (2006) transitioned the conversation from focusing on the achievement gap to focusing on our educational debt. When we focus on a gap, it is plausible to target the underperformers. However, an educational debt puts the burden of responsibility on us, the adults in society. Furthermore, framing the educational disparity as a debt highlights the array of negative social burdens that accumulate for children (Rothstein, 2004).

It is incumbent on educators everywhere to "promote a brave policy of interrogating [their] *own* roles in producing inequitable racial orders" so that the next steps in atoning for deficiencies can begin (Pollock, 2004, p. 218, emphasis in the original). We must increase opportunities for early childhood education, and there must be intentional efforts to recruit, educate, and employ highly skilled educators of color. We must drastically decrease our classroom sizes. We must teach parents how they can help educate their children; if the

Next Steps for the Reader

- Identify the closest public and private schools to your home. Research each institution's test performance, spending per pupil, racial composition, and SES level. If determining the SES level is difficult, look at the number of students who are on free or reduced lunch as an SES indicator. What differences are there between the schools? Inquire whether you can tour each school.

- Research the statutes guiding discipline for schools in your area. Are schools required to track data on discipline and disaggregate them by race? Is corporal punishment allowed? When must parents or guardians be informed about discipline of their child? What processes must be followed for a student to be suspended or dismissed from school?

Additional Resources for Up-to-Date Facts and Stats

Annie E. Casey Foundation
- Education—http://www.aecf.org/KnowledgeCenter/Education.aspx
- Kids Count Data Center—http://datacenter.kidscount.org/

Center for Effective Discipline
- Homepage—http://www.stophitting.com/
- Discipline at School—http://www.stophitting.com/index.php?page=atschool-main

Childcare.gov: Forum on Child and Family Statistics
- Homepage—http://www.childstats.gov/

Data Accountability Center: Individuals With Disabilities Education Act (IDEA) Data
- Homepage—https://www.ideadata.org/
- Population and Enrollment Data—https://www.ideadata.org/PopulationData.asp

National Center for Education Statistics
- Homepage—http://nces.ed.gov/
- NAEP Assessment—http://nces.ed.gov/nationsreportcard/

UNICEF Childinfo
- Education—http://www.childinfo.org/education.html

U.S. Department of Education
- Homepage—http://www.ed.gov/
- Civil Rights Data Collection—http://ocrdata.ed.gov/
- Office of Special Education and Rehabilitative Services—http://www2.ed.gov/about/offices/list/osers/

parents are a product of our broken educational system, how can we expect them to know how to support their own children's education? We must grant children access to enriching cocurricular activities. Much student learning occurs outside the classroom, and we must offer a host of educational, life-affirming opportunities.

Failing in this regard carries a cost, not only for children, but also for society as a whole. The children forgotten today will become the adults we cannot ignore tomorrow. These adults will have kids of their own, locking us into a vicious negative feedback cycle followed generation after generation.

REFERENCES

Allington, R. L., & McGill-Franzen, A. (2003). The impact of summer setback on the reading achievement gap. *Phi Delta Kappan, 85*(1), 68–75.

Ansalone, G. (2009). *Exploring unequal achievement in the schools: The social construction of failure.* Lanham, MD: Rowman & Littlefield.

Barton, P. E. (2003). *Parsing the achievement gap: Baselines for tracking progress.* Educational Testing Service. Retrieved from http://www.ets.org/Media/Education_Topics/pdf/parsing.pdf

Barton, P. E., & Coley, R. J. (2009). *Parsing the achievement gap II.* Educational Testing Service. Retrieved from http://www.ets.org/Media/Research/pdf/PICPARSINGII.pdf

Blanchett, W. J. (2006). Disproportionate representation of African American students in special education: Acknowledging the role of white privilege and racism. *Educational Researcher, 35*(6), 24–28.

Cameron, M., & Sheppard, S. M. (2006). School discipline and social work practice: Application of research and theory to intervention. *Children & Schools, 28*(1), 15–22.

Center for Effective Discipline (CED). (n.d.). *U.S.: Corporal punishment and paddling statistics by state and race.* Retrieved from http://www.stophitting.com/index.php?page=statesbanning

ChildStats.gov. (2009). *Demographic background.* Retrieved from http://www.childstats.gov/americaschildren/index3.asp

Clotfelter, C. T., Ladd, H. F., & Vigdor, J. (2005). Who teaches whom? Race and the distribution of novice teachers. *Economics of Education Review, 24*(4), 377–392.

Cooper, R. (2010). *Those who can, teach* (12th ed.). Boston, MA: Wadsworth Cengage Learning.

Crowley, S. (2003). The affordable housing crisis: Residential mobility of poor families and school mobility of poor children. *The Journal of Negro Education, 72*(1), 22–38.

Denson, K. (2004). Minimizing the effects of student mobility through teacher and administrator training. In R. B. Cooter (Ed.), *Perspectives on rescuing urban literacy education: Spies, saboteurs, and saints* (pp. 117–134). Mahwah, NJ: Lawrence Erlbaum.

Dowker, A. (2005). *Individual differences in arithmetic: Implications for psychology, neuroscience and education.* New York: Psychology Press.

Fenning, P., & Rose, J. (2007). Overrepresentation of African American students in exclusionary discipline: The role of school policy. *Urban Education, 42*(6), 536–559.

Ferri, B. A., & Connor, D. J. (2005a). Tools of exclusion—Race, disability, and (re) segregated education. *Teachers College Record, 107*(3), 453–474.

Ferri, B. A., & Connor, D. J. (2005b). In the shadow of Brown: Special education and overrepresentation of students of color. *Remedial and Special Education, 26,* 92, 93–100.

Freeman, C. E., Scafidi, B., & Sjoquist, D. L. (2005). Racial segregation in Georgia public schools, 1994–2001: Trends, causes, and impact on teacher quality. In J. C. Boger & G. Orfield (Eds.), *School resegregation: Must the South turn back?* (pp. 148–163). Chapel Hill, NC: University of North Carolina Press.

Giroux, H. A., & Schmidt, M. (2004). Closing the achievement gap: A metaphor for children left behind. *Journal of Educational Change, 5,* 213–228.

Global Initiative to End All Corporal Punishment of Children. (2009, November). *Global progress towards prohibiting all corporal punishment.* Retrieved from http://www.endcorporalpunishment.org/pages/pdfs/charts/Chart-Glob al.pdf

Goodman, J. F. (2006). School discipline in moral disarray. *The Journal of Moral Education, 35*(2), 213–230.

Gottfredson, G. D., Gottfredson, D. C., Payne, A. A., & Gottfredson, N. C. (2005). School climate predictors of school disorder: Results from a national study of delinquency prevention in schools. *Journal of Research in Crime and Delinquency, 42*(4), 412–444.

Gravois, T. D., & Rosenfield, S. A. (2006). Impact of instructional consultation teams on the disproportionate referral and placement of minority students in special education. *Remedial and Special Education, 27*(1), 42–52.

Harris, D. N., & Herrington, C. D. (2006). Accountability, standards, and the growing achievement gap: Lessons from the past half-century. *American Journal of Education, 112,* 209–238.

Harry, B., & Klingner, J. K. (2005). *Why are so many minority students in special education? Understanding race & disability in schools.* New York: Teacher College Press.

Hartman, C., & Leff, A. (2006). High classroom turnover: How some children get left behind. In C. Hartman (Ed.), *Poverty and race in America: The emerging agendas* (pp. 269–272). Lanham, MD: Rowman & Littlefield.

Holcomb-McCoy, C. (2007). *School counseling to close the achievement gap: A social justice framework for success.* Thousand Oaks, CA: Corwin Press.

Hunter, R. C., & Bartee, R. (2003). The achievement gap: Issues of competition, class, and race. *Education and Urban Society, 35*(2), 151–160.

Johnston, R. C. (2000, March 15). Who is "Asian"? Cultural differences defy simple categories. *Education Week, 19*(27). Retrieved from http://eric.ed.gov/ERICDocs/data/ericdocs2sql/content_storage_e01/0000019b/80/19/5f/3d.pdf

Johnston, R. C., & Viadero, V. (2000, March 15). Unmet promise: Raising minority achievement. *Education Week, 19*(27). Retrieved from http://eric.ed.gov/ERICDocs/data/ericdocs2sql/content_storage_01/0000019b/80/19/5f/3d.pdf

Julianelle, P. F., & Foscarinis, M. (2003). Responding to the school mobility of children and youth experiencing homelessness: The McKinney-Vento Act and beyond. *The Journal of Negro Education, 72*(1), 39–54.

Karapurkar Bhasin, T., Brocksen, S., Nonkin Avchen, R., & Van Naarden Braun, K. (2006). Prevalence of four developmental disabilities among children aged 8 years: Metropolitan Atlanta developmental disabilities surveillance program, 1996 and 2000. *Surveillance Summaries, 55*(No. SS-1), 1–9.

Kober, N. (2001, April). *It takes more than testing: Closing the achievement gap*. Washington, DC: Center on Education Policy.

Kozol, J. (2005). *The shame of a nation: The restoration of apartheid schooling in America*. New York: Crown Publishers.

Ladson-Billings, G. (2006). From the achievement gap to the education debt: Understanding achievement in U.S. Schools. *Educational Researcher, 35*(7), 3–12.

Lee, J. (2002). Racial and ethnic achievement gap trends: Reversing the progress toward equity? *Educational Researcher, 31*(1), 3–12.

Lee, J. S., & Bowen, N. K. (2006). Parent involvement, cultural capital, and achievement gap among elementary school children. *American Educational Research Journal, 43*(2), 193–218.

Manning, J. B., & Kovach, J. A. (2003). The continuing challenge of excellence and equity. In B. Williams (Ed.), *Closing the achievement gap: A vision for changing beliefs and practices* (pp. 25–47). Alexandria, VA: Association for Supervision & Curriculum Development.

McKown, C., & Weinstein, R. S. (2008). Teacher expectations, classroom context, and the achievement gap. *Journal of School Psychology, 46*(3), 235–261.

Monroe, C. R. (2005). Why are "bad boys" always Black? Causes of disproportionality in school discipline and recommendations for change. *The Clearing House, 79*(1), 45–50.

Morris, E. W. (2005). "Tuck in that shirt!" Race, class, gender, and discipline in an urban school. *Sociological Perspectives, 48*(1), 25–48.

National Assessment of Educational Progress (NAEP). (n.d.). *The NAEP glossary of terms*. Retrieved from http://nationsreportcard.gov/glossary.asp#p

National Assessment of Educational Progress (NAEP). (2005). *The NAEP reading achievement levels by grade*. Retrieved from http://nces.ed.gov/nationsreportcard/reading/achieveall.asp#grade4

National Assessment of Educational Progress (NAEP). (2006). *The NAEP mathematics achievement levels by grade*. Retrieved from http://nces.ed.gov/nationsreportcard/mathematics/achieveall.asp

National Assessment of Educational Progress (NAEP). (2009, November 10). *NAEP overview*. Retrieved from http://nces.ed.gov/nationsreportcard/about/

National Center for Education Statistics (NCES). (n.d.). *NAEP data explorer*. Retrieved from http://nces.ed.gov/nationsreportcard/naepdata/dataset.aspx

National Center for Education Statistics (NCES). (2007). *The nation's report card: Reading 2007*. Retrieved from http://nces.ed.gov/nationsreportcard/pdf/main2007/2007496.pdf

National Center for Education Statistics (NCES). (2009). *The nation's report card: Mathematics 2009*. Retrieved from http://nationsreportcard.gov/math_2009/math_2009_report/pdf/mathematics_2009.pdf

Neuman, S. B. (2005). The knowledge gap: Implications for early education. In D. K. Dickinson & S. B. Neuman (Eds.), *Handbook of early literacy research, Volume 2* (pp. 29–40). New York: Guilford.

Norman, O., Ault, C. R., Bentz, B., & Meskimen, L. (2001). The Black-White "achievement gap" as a perennial challenge of urban science education: A sociocultural and historical overview with implications for research and practice. *Journal of Research in Science Teaching, 38*(10), 1101–1114.

O'Connor, C., & DeLuca Fernandez, S. (2006). Race, class, and disproportionality: Reevaluating the relationship between poverty and special education placement. *Educational Researcher, 35*(6), 6–11.

Owen, S. S. (2005). The relationship between social capital and corporal punishment in schools. *Youth & Society, 37*(1), 85–112.

Pastor, P. N., & Reuben, C. A. (2005). Racial and ethnic differences in ADHD and LD in young school-age children: Parental reports in the National Health Interview Survey. *Public Health Records, 120,* 383–392.

Pastor, P. N., Reuben, C. A., & Loeb, M. (2009). Functional difficulties among school-aged children: United States, 2001–2007. *National Health Statistics Report, 19,* 1–24.

Pollock, M. (2004). *Colormute: Race talk dilemmas in an American school*. Princeton, NJ: Princeton University Press.

Rhodes, R. L., Ochoa, S. H., & Ortiz, S. O. (2005). *Assessing culturally and linguistically diverse students: A practical guide.* New York: Guilford.

Rothstein, R. (2004). The achievement gap: Closing the achievement gap requires more than just improving schools. *Educational leadership.* Retrieved from http://bsdweb.bsdvt.org/district/EquityExcellence/Research/Rothst einAchievementGap.pdf

Rumberger, R. W. (2003). The causes and consequences of student mobility. *The Journal of Negro Education, 72*(1), 6–21.

Sacks, P. (2007). *Tearing down the gates: Confronting the class divide in American education.* Los Angeles: University of California Press.

Sheldon, S. B., & Epstein, J. L. (2005). Involvement counts: Family and community partnerships and mathematics achievement. *The Journal of Educational Research, 98*(4), 196–207.

Simon, B. S. (2008). Predictors and effects of family involvement in high schools. In J. L. Epstein (Ed.), *School, family, and community partnerships: Your handbook for action* (3rd ed., pp. 211–219). Thousand Oaks, CA: Corwin Press.

Singham, M. (2003). The achievement gap: Myths and reality. *Phi Delta Kappan, 84*(8), 586–591.

Skiba, R. J., Michael, R. S., Nardo, A. C., & Peterson, R. L. (2002). The color of discipline: Sources of racial and gender disproportionality in school punishment. *The Urban Review, 34*(4), 317–342.

Skiba, R., Poloni-Staudinger, L., Simmons, A. B., Feggins-Azziz, L. R., & Chung, C. G. (2005). Unproven links: Can poverty explain ethnic disproportionality in special education. *The Journal of Special Education, 39*(3), 130–144.

Tenenbaum, H. R., & Ruck, M. D. (2007). Are teachers' expectations different for racial minority than for European American students? A meta-analysis. *Journal of Educational Psychology, 99*(2), 253–273.

U.S. Department of Education. (2006). *2006 national and state projections.* Retrieved from http://ocrdata.ed.gov/Projections_2006.aspx

Wagner, M., Kutash, K., Duchnowski, A. J., Epstein, M. H., & Sumi, W. C. (2005). The children and youth we serve: A national picture of the characteristics of students with emotional disturbances receiving special education. *Journal of Emotional and Behavioral Disorders, 13*(2), 79–96.

6

The Leaky Pipeline
Access to Higher Education

WHETHER IT IS FOLLOWING A DELIVERY OR AN adoption process, parents' first hope for their child is good health. Ten fingers, ten toes, a heartbeat, and a healthy cry seem like the most important things on Earth. However, hopes for a child do not remain centered on health for too long; in wanting their children to have successful and fulfilling lives, parents know that higher education is crucial. Whether at a college or university, higher education is the most likely path to success in the United States.

A college degree is a valuable commodity. Aside from the role it plays in helping people lead richer and fuller lives, education also increases opportunities for higher earnings over a lifetime.

Figure 6.1 reflects the entire U.S. population. In dissecting further, people between 25 and 35 years old make, on average, $10,000 more per year in salary when they have a bachelor's degree as opposed to a high school diploma. That salary difference is more than $20,000 per year for people 35–44 years old (Baum, Payea, & Steele, 2006). As these yearly disparities accumulate, we can estimate that a person with a high school diploma will make $1.2 million throughout his or her life compared to someone with a bachelor's degree who will bring home $2.1 million (Cheeseman Day & Newburger, 2002). This drastic difference in earning potential makes obtaining a degree even from the most expensive institution a sound economic investment.

Having a degree from a higher education institution also provides job security. In tough economic times, there is a lot of discussion about the unemployment rate. However, joblessness is not a burden that is shared equally. For the 25 and older population, in November 2010, 15.2% of those without a high school diploma were unemployed, followed by 9.6% of those with a high school diploma and 4.5% for individuals with a bachelor's degree or higher (U.S. Bureau of Labor Statistics, 2010).

It would be unfair to continue without highlighting another disparity in these data, a disparity highlighted throughout this book—race. It is not just having a degree that earns the big bucks. As seen in Figure 6.2, earning a degree and being White provides the greatest possibility for increasing human and social capital.

In 2007, Whites with a bachelor's degree earned, on average, $58,652 per year. This is a little over $12,000 more a year than Blacks and nearly $14,000 more a year than Hispanics with the same degree. There were not enough Hispanics with doctorates represented in this data set to report results in that column (U.S. Census Bureau, 2010).

Students of color have many hurdles to overcome on the journey toward earning a college degree. The preceding chapters highlighted many of these obstacles, but there are distinctive hurdles inherent to higher

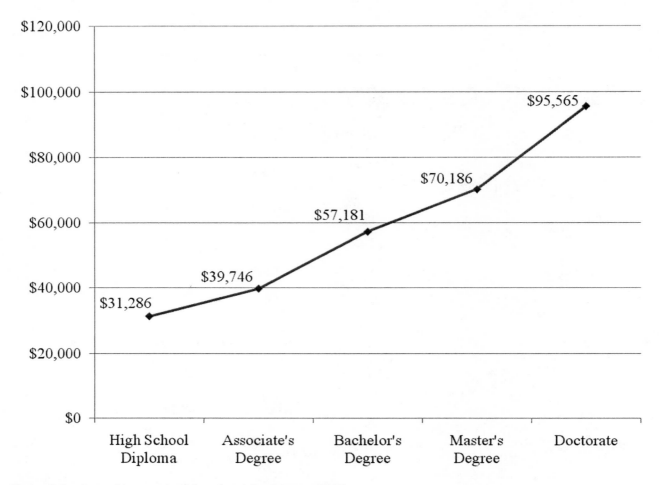

Figure 6.1   Annual Income by Educational Attainment, 2007

(U.S. Census Bureau, 2010)

education. All told, this can make for long odds of success.

> We know that for every 100 students in the U.S. who begin ninth grade, 67 finish high school in four years; 38 go to college and only 18 earn an associate's degree within three years or a bachelor's degree in six years. Underserved students [e.g., students of color] predominate among those who are lost along the educational pipeline. (Pathways to College Network, 2003, p. 10)

Higher education plays its own role in ensuring that the status quo remains. Examples abound, including data drawn from standardized tests like the SAT, and a substantial portion of this chapter is devoted to this topic. There are other important access variables, including attacks on affirmative action, legacy admis-

sions, and covert admissions tools in the hands of the privileged, such as private admissions consultants.

~~Scholastic Aptitude Test~~ ~~Scholastic Assessment Test~~ SAT Reasoning Test

The SAT Reasoning Test (SAT) was taken by 1,530,128 college hopefuls in 2009 (College Board, 2009). The outcomes of this assessment weigh heavily on the future hopes and dreams of the college-bound. Scoring well can put a person on the track to college success; not doing so can instantly derail progress. In terms of college acceptance, the hours spent taking this test can be just as important as the sum total of all the time a child has spent in school. This reality exists despite the overwhelming evidence that the SAT is nothing more than

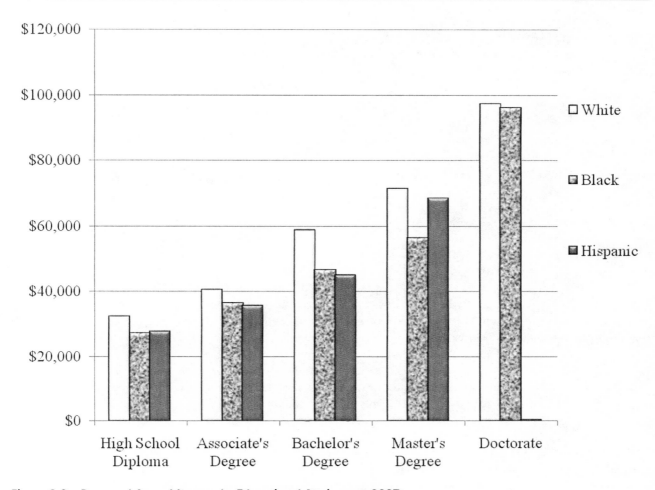

Figure 6.2   Race and Annual Income by Educational Attainment, 2007

(U.S. Census Bureau, 2010)

a measure of the discrimination students of color continually experience.

The SAT has received much criticism for purporting to measure intelligence and aptitude and asserting itself as an accurate predictor of college performance. Each time the SAT's suppositions regarding what this test *actually* measures are shown to be false, the name of the test is changed. As highlighted by the subsection title, it went from the Scholastic Aptitude Test to the Scholastic Assessment Test to, currently, the SAT Reasoning Test (Whiston, 2009). S-A-T is no longer an acronym for anything; it is just a brand for marketing. There is "an important truth about the history of racism and science—if the facts do not support theories of racial inequality, just alter the study or change the facts" (Fluehr-Lobban, 2006, p. 140). This altering and changing has occurred throughout the history of the SAT. The data to follow support this assertion.

The current version of the SAT published by the College Board consists of three sections: Critical Reading, Mathematics, and Writing, with a scoring range of 200–800. The averages of the 1,530,128 college-bound high school seniors who took the exam in 2009 are in Table 6.1 (College Board, 2009).

These scores are broken down further by several demographic categories. Table 6.2 depicts the racial breakdown for these 2009 test scores.

As represented in Table 6.2, there are racial differences in performance on the SAT. Most notable is the

TABLE 6.1	
SAT Average Scores, 2009 (College Board, 2009)	
Critical Reading	501
Mathematics	515
Writing	493

TABLE 6.2			
SAT Scores by Race, 2009 (College Board, 2009)			
2009 SAT Scores Racial Breakdown			
	Critical Reading	*Mathematics*	*Writing*
American Indian or Alaska Native	486	493	469
Asian, Asian American, or Pacific Islander	516	587	520
Black or African American	429	426	421
Mexican or Mexican American	453	463	446
Puerto Rican	452	450	443
Other Hispanics, Latino, or Latin American	455	461	448
White	528	536	517

wide achievement gap between Black and White students. There is an average disparity among the three test sections of 102 points. The Mexican–White disparity gap averages at 73 points on the three sections. It is centrally important to highlight that the College Board purports that a 60-point variation between students represents a viable difference in ability (College Board, 2009).

Where there are racial differences, we often find a covarying SES dynamic. In regard to the SAT, this is also true. Table 6.3 samples the differences in SAT score as they pertain to family income.

From families making $20,000 and less per year to those making in excess of $200,000, the average disparity on the three sections is 127 points. A 60-point gap represents a viable difference, and these test scores are twice that threshold (College Board, 2009). However, while the influence of SES is an important conversation to have, it must not disengage us from our focus on race. As Thomas Kane (1998) argues, even these SES data do not outweigh race in decisions on college admissions. Even poor Whites have advantages in collegiate admissions over poor people of color.

To explore these advantages, Theodore Micceri (2007) examined the admissions files for 11 public universities in Florida and their first-generation college applicants with high school GPAs of 2.5–4.5, from summer 1997 through spring 2006. In a sample of 628,946 students, the results show succinctly that it is more often advantageous to be White and male. Even when compared to students with the same high school GPA, White males outperform their peers more often than not. Again, since the College Board deems a 60-point differential between scores a viable difference in ability, the differences found are noteworthy. In one example from Table 6.4, Black males with a 4.5 GPA have an average SAT score of 1206. White males with the exact same GPA scored 1319 on the SAT. That is a disparity of 113 points, nearly double the number of points the SAT requires to deem that these high school students have different abilities (Micceri, 2007).

Table 6.4 is a behemoth of a data set; however, we can make meaning of these numbers in two ways. First, within each GPA section the racial disparity is easily noted. In theory, students who have similar

TABLE 6.3			
SAT Scores by SES, 2009 (College Board, 2009)			
2009 SAT Scores Selected SES Breakdown			
	Critical Reading	*Mathematics*	*Writing*
> $20,000	434	457	430
$40,000–$60,000	488	497	476
$80,000–$100,000	517	528	505
$120,000–$140,000	529	542	520
$160,000–$200,000	542	554	535
$200,000 >	563	579	560

TABLE 6.4
SAT Scores by Race, Gender, and High School GPA (Micceri, 2007)

	2.5 GPA		3.0 GPA		3.5 GPA		4.0 GPA		4.5 GPA	
	Male	Female	Male	Female	Male	Female	Male	Female	Male	Female
White	1042	971	1082	1016	1148	1083	1226	1162	1319	1255
Black	909	843	964	903	1040	967	1118	1067	1206	1175
Hispanic	986	914	1011	955	1089	1023	1158	1099	1273	1208
Asian	998	946	1047	989	1119	1062	1211	1140	1330	1277

GPAs should score similarly on the SAT. Just looking at those with a 4.0 GPA, Black women score far below (95 points) White women. Also, in the same GPA category, Hispanic men score significantly below (68 points) White men (Micceri, 2007).

Another way Table 6.4 can be used is to compare across GPA categories. Leaving race out of the equation, the average person would guess that a student with a 3.5 GPA would score higher on the SAT than a student with a 2.5 GPA. Across both genders, Black students

with a 3.5 GPA score lower on the SAT than Whites with a 2.5 GPA. These differences are not substantial, but that they even exist is noteworthy (Micceri, 2007).

The research clearly shows that Whites answer more questions correctly than do Blacks and Chicano/as (the term *Chicano/as* was used in this particular research article). That is true for both the verbal and math sections. However, this is not because people of color are more likely to do poorly on tests. This disparity is created by a confusing set of events where Whites are more

Question #1

The actor's bearing on stage seemed _____; her movements were natural and her technique _____.

a. unremitting...blasé
b. fluid...tentative
c. unstudied...uncontrived
d. eclectic...uniform
e. grandiose...controlled

Question #2

The dance company rejects _____, preferring to present only _____ dances in a manner that underscores their traditional appeal.

a. invention...emergent
b. fidelity...long-maligned
c. ceremony...ritualistic
d. innovation...time-honored
e. custom...ancient

Figure 6.3   Example SAT Verbal Questions, Racial Difference

(Kidder & Rosner, 2002/2003, p. 152)

likely to be given questions they have a propensity to answer correctly (Kidder & Rosner, 2002–2003).

This is a complex point, but scholars William Kidder and Jay Rosner (2002–2003) break this down into digestible parts. When students take the SAT, they answer test questions that will never be a part of their actual score. These questions are present so the College Board can determine which questions should be used in the future. Figure 6.3 contains two such sample questions from the verbal section of an old SAT.

The correct answer to the first question is C, and the correct answer to the second is D. On the surface, there does not appear to be any overt difference in the substance of these questions that would lead someone to believe there is bias present. However, 8% more Black students answered question #1 correctly than did White students, and 24% more White students answered question #2 correctly than did Black students. Herein is where the SAT injects bias; Question #1 was rejected as a possible question for the SAT while question #2 was accepted (Kidder & Rosner, 2002–2003).

There is a simple reason why these decisions are made and it reflects a "tyranny of the majority." One of the primary mechanisms for determining whether a question makes it onto the SAT is a measure called reliability, a rating based on how well the question sorts high-achieving from low-achieving students. A question that tends to be answered correctly by high-achieving students and incorrectly by low-achieving students would be considered a reliable measure. While this does not appear racist, this process requires that the test be normed to a specific population, in this case, the general population of the United States. Since Whites are the majority of test takers in the United States, their correct answers set the norm for reliability. With so many more Whites taking the SAT, the questions they answer correctly appear reliable, while the smaller number of people of color who answer a question correctly appear as an anomaly, resulting in the question being deleted from the exam (Kidder & Rosner, 2002–2003). As questioned further by the researchers:

> While the content of both items [exampled previously] is ostensibly neutral, can it be said that the SAT is truly unbiased if, time and time again, the test construction process tends to prefer (for statistical reasons) items like [question #2] (that favors Whites), and rejects items like [question #1] (that favors African Americans)? (Kidder & Rosner, 2002/2003, p. 155)

Of course, the answer is no. We cannot pretend the SAT is neutral when bias influences question selection.

There is additional evidence asserting the SAT measures factors besides academic prowess, most notably the skills of those deemed to be good test takers and the cultural knowledge students may bring with them into the exam. One research team investigated such notions by examining the reading comprehension section of the SAT. This section is comprised of reading several paragraphs of text and then answering questions directly related to the text. The College Board asserts that test takers do not require any background knowledge on the subject matter of the reading passages; they must simply be able to read the information, digest its meaning, and answer questions correctly. The researchers drew a sample of 136 students from an introductory psychology research pool and two honors sections of the same course. These college students took a test of 100 reading comprehension questions from the SAT. However, only 58 students were given the reading passages associated with the test questions. The other 78 students were simply given the questions, omitting the reading passages. Given that each question is multiple choice with five possible answers, based on pure chance, the average score should be 20%. What was actually found is in Table 6.5 (Katz, Lautenschlager, Blackburn, & Harris, 1990).

Obviously, it is advantageous to receive the reading comprehension passages. However, why did the group that did not receive the reading passages score 17.6% higher than we would assume if they were simply guessing at correct answers? The reason this occurred is that the SAT measures more than comprehension.

TABLE 6.5 SAT Reading Comprehension Experimentation (Katz et al., 1990)	Average number of correct answers (100 questions)
Received Reading Comprehension Passage	56.8
Did Not Receive Passage	37.6

What students carry in beyond pencils affects the test outcomes. When the researchers used the same experimental design with college honors students, the correct answer average was 46.6% for those without the reading passages (Katz et al., 1990).

This introduces the idea that testing draws from life experience, skills, and culture—all of which vary depending on social location. One author stated, "Culture is not merely a body of knowledge and skills. It is also a set of strategies for dealing with the unknown and with tasks that seem difficult" (Jencks, 1998, p. 69). We can take this argument even further by stating that all knowledge carries culture with it. As such, all knowledge is cultural knowledge, making any assessment a test not only of material, but also of one's knowledge of the cultural context of the material. Amado Padilla and Graciela Borsato argue, "Neglect of the role of the sociocultural context in which testing takes place absolutely collides with the ideal of equity in assessment" (2008, p. 6). Moreover, if more proof is required as to how culture infuses assessments, in 2011 the SAT came under heavy criticism for a question asking students to reflect on the realism and impact of reality TV. Ironically, those who study hardest for the SAT are probably the least likely to have spent significant time watching reality television, soaking up that culturally laden knowledge (Steinberg, 2011).

Sadly, there is one piece of U.S. culture that students of color do take with them into the administration of any test—our long history of racism. This is exemplified through the research on stereotype threat, a phenomenon whereby people of color perform poorly on exams when they feel they are being evaluated by a racist stereotype. In one study, 20 Black female and 20 White female undergraduate students were interspersed and divided into two groups, both of which would take the same exam. However, the first group was told it was going to be administered a test measuring intellectual ability, and the second group was told this was merely a problem-solving assignment. The results were astounding. Black undergraduates in the first group performed worse than those in the second ($p < .01$). A belief that one is being judged as intellectually inferior may have triggered the stereotype threat effect and lowered the Black students' performance (Steele & Aronson, 1998).

Another study of undergraduate students examined whether the racial response could be primed. Two groups of White and Black students were again ad-

ministered an exam. Members of the first group were asked their race before the exam; those in the second group were asked their race following the exam. Again, the first group of Black students performed much worse to a statistically significant level. Additionally, the Black and White students in group two who did not receive the demographic question prior to the test performed at the same level. The simple action of asking a person's race was enough to trigger stereotype threat (Steele & Aronson, 1998). Such studies show how deeply buried stereotypes are and how they can affect the test performance of an otherwise outstanding student.

The SAT has serious problems associated with its design and use; the issues relating to students of color are enough of a reason for colleges and universities to rethink using such assessments. Some universities are doing just this. I take great personal pride that in 2011, my institution, DePaul University, became the largest private institution in the United States to be test-optional for undergraduate admissions. Prospective students do not need to submit an SAT or ACT score to be considered for admission. Instead, DePaul uses other admission materials, including essays (Hoover, 2011).

College Admissions

There is perhaps no more controversial and misunderstood entity in higher education than affirmative action. It has a long, muddy case history and is a subject that elicits strong visceral reactions. But in terms of college admissions, it is something we cannot ignore.

Affirmative action, as an idea, was first used during the Great Depression as part of the National Labor Relations Act (NLRA) of 1935. This legislation sought to empower the National Labor Relations Board to set right the chronic discrimination in hiring and payment practices "by ordering affirmative action" (Turner, 1990, p. 5). This Act saw discrimination in any form of hiring or employment as a slight against what the United States aimed to be. Affirmative action was meant to right a wrong, to level playing fields, and to give those long denied opportunities equal footing (Foner, 1997; Katznelson, 2005).

Affirmative action cases in higher education have been working through the court system for decades. Finally, in 2003, two cases came before the U.S. Supreme

Court, both involving the University of Michigan. *Gratz v. Bollinger* (2003) involved an undergraduate admissions affirmative action program that awarded points to students for various attributes, one of which was race. In this case, the High Court ruled the points system violated citizens' rights to equal protection under the law as dictated by the Fourteenth Amendment to the Constitution. Therefore, the points system was not deemed a legal affirmative action program. The second case, *Grutter v. Bollinger* (2003), centered on the admission practices of the law school. The law school considered race in admission decisions, but such consideration did not encompass a numerical or otherwise tangible process. Race was merely one of many factors incorporated in the admission discussions. The Supreme Court affirmed that inclusion of race is legally allowable as long as the use of race was finite and focused.

The purpose of this section is not to debate affirmative action in general or to delve into the tenets of these specific cases. Instead, I choose to focus on the irony present in this debate. I agree with much of the reasoning and wording of both of these Supreme Court decisions. I believe university officials should be allowed to use race as one factor in admission decisions. The process set up by the University of Michigan's law school represents a best practice in how a university can undertake such a process. The strongest tool higher education faculty and staff have at their disposal is professional judgment earned through extensive educational achievement (earning undergraduate, graduate, and doctoral degrees) and through the experience they have accumulated while serving at colleges and universities. The Supreme Court implicitly granted deference to the admissions program of the law school based largely on its earned professional judgment to make these decisions. However, when the undergraduate admissions program attempted to quantify admissions decisions by creating a point system, it gave away much of its defense of professional judgment. There is no viable defense for why race was attributed 20 points, as it was, in this admissions process. Why not 18? Why not 22? Where did 20 come from? Leaving one open to such questions throws the door open to having your entire process completely dismantled.

While I am not a fan of these point systems, there is an irony to be exposed. The *Gratz* case focused solely on how the points attributed to race unfairly tipped the scales for admission. All told, under this formerly employed admission process, a student could earn 150 points. Of these points, academic achievement comprised 110, 73% of the points possible. Race could account for 20 points, only 13% of the possible points. Race was but a small sliver of this pie. However, I can still see how individuals could raise concern over these 20 points. After all, these points could be a final determining factor. But if that is the case, why did the *Gratz* lawsuit fail to challenge the other nonacademic points that were attributed to applicants? The following are a few other areas that earned applicants admission points to the University of Michigan:

- 10 points to Michigan residents and an additional six if the student lives in an underrepresented county in the state, such as the upper peninsula;
- four or five points if the student is a legacy;
- 20 points if the family is of a lower socioeconomic status;
- five points if the applicant is a man and wants to enter the field of nursing;
- 20 points for a scholarship athlete; and
- 20 points can be applied at the discretion of the Provost (Ballantine & Roberts, 2009; University of Michigan, 2003).

Why is race such a lightning rod? Clearly geographical affirmative action does not bother anyone. In addition, the preference given to some athletes, the poor, or men serving in a female-dominated field does not raise concern. It is particularly surprising that the Provost discretionary points have gone unnoticed for so long. Such discretionary points are used all over the country to grant admission to the children of politicians and wealthy financial donors. The University of Illinois at Urbana-Champaign recently exemplified how such powerful mechanisms can influence admission decisions. In 2009, a major exposé highlighted how politicians regularly influenced admission decisions at Illinois's premiere public higher education institution. This reality was so commonplace, the Admissions Office had a special name for these cases—"Category I" applicants (St. Clair, Cohen, & Becker, 2009). While the University of Illinois has since stopped this practice and is reviewing all of its admissions processes, the taint of this scandal will be felt there for years to come (St. Clair & Cohen, 2009).

Yet, while the issues at the University of Illinois are troubling, the university acted covertly, in secrecy, because it knew it was doing something unethical. In other areas, factors affecting admission are treated as public knowledge. Legacy admissions are one such case. A legacy admission process is a tool to ensure that those who have achieved previously can set their children up to achieve in the future. These applicants receive admission, in some cases, regardless of aptitude. Also, these students have often already had access to nearly every other advantage in life, from good schools, adequate health care, and favorable treatment in the justice system, to drinking cleaner water and breathing cleaner air. Where is the outrage about these policies?

It is the elite institutions across the United States that have the most pronounced legacy admissions. Moreover, these elite institutions educate many of this nation's leaders. Over the past 105 years, up until 2008, 47 of those years had a president in the White House who had a degree from Harvard, Yale, or Princeton (Karabel, 2006). If we look through 2012, with President Obama being a Harvard law graduate, this becomes 51 out of the last 105 years.

Elite colleges and universities will defend their legacy admits, arguing these admissions enable them to gain favor with wealthy donors and those in powerful positions. This helps the institution in many regards. Duke University, for instance, self-reported it admits 100–125 students each year based on the wealth and connections of the students' family (Schmidt, 2007). The wealth and connections of these families enables Duke to pursue its mission of education. In making these decisions, institutions like Duke are making an end justify the means argument. While their actions perpetuate privilege, they feel justified because they are seeking to serve the greater institution.

Regardless of how admissions decisions are justified, legacy admits represent a sizeable portion of the freshman class at elite schools across the country. In 2004, Harvard University admitted roughly 11% of its total applicant pool. This low acceptance rate reflects the prestige of the institution; many of the best and brightest are not admitted. However, of those admitted to Harvard, approximately 40% were legacies. It does not stop at Harvard or even the Ivy League; at Notre Dame, 23% of the entire school is legacy students (Schmidt, 2007).

Colleges and universities might be able to argue in favor of legacy admissions if these admits were stellar students. An Office of Civil Rights study found that Harvard legacy admits performed lower on nearly every standard when compared to their nonlegacy counterparts. Another study reported that legacy status equated to a 160-point increase in an SAT score when being considered for admission. With this nation's long history of racial discrimination, it is important to remember that many legacy lineages began when these schools only admitted White men. Linking back to affirmative action, with all of the lawsuits over admission decisions taking race into account, at least one author argues, "if anyone is winning the war over college affirmative action, it's wealthy white kids" (Schmidt, 2007, p. 6).

Aside from legacy admissions, still other admission tools are available to college hopefuls. There are organizations and consultants who seek to propel high school students into their desired college or university for a fee. However, many have questioned the ethics of such organizations.

> Under the pretense of fair competition, tens of thousands of high school students and their families employ the scholastic equivalent of steroids—test-prep courses, private consultants, Internet mills for massaging if not entirely creating their essays, exaggerated or cynical accounts of their community service. (Freedman, 2006, p. 9)

There are as many as 4,000–5,000 individual consultants across the United States who provide such assistance (Bick, 2008). In 2006, approximately 120,000 college hopefuls used their services (Boccela, 2007). Samuel Freedman (2006) likened the use of consultants to the performance-enhancing drug use and abuse in Major League Baseball. For example, in the case of Barry Bonds, we have a man with gifted ability. He was born with a skill level for baseball that was far and above that of many elite athletes. Nevertheless, he, like many others, still saw a reason to (allegedly) give himself a boost through performance-enhancing drugs. The use of college consultants is very similar because those seeking such services are often those who were born into a privileged position in society. They already attend good schools and have families who have the money to pay (sometimes significant amounts) for these extra services.

Admission consultation with an online professional can cost $299 (Boccela, 2007). However, an average hourly rate is $160 (Bick, 2008), with private consultants billing on average $3,300 for a full package of their services (Freedman, 2006). If your child wishes to take a year off between high school and college, there are even gap-year consultants who can be hired for $1,000–$2,000. They ensure that the student uses the time off in a meaningful way so the experience is attractive to colleges and universities (Shapira, 2007). However, as we get into the upper echelons of admissions consultation, there is further stratification. Better-known entities, such as an organization called IvyWise, can bill anywhere from $10,000–$30,000 for their services (Freedman, 2006). Perhaps the most notorious fixture in the field is Michele Hernandez. As a former admissions representative at Dartmouth College and author of the highly recognized book, *A Is for Admission: The Insider's Guide to Getting Into the Ivy League and Other Top Colleges*, she offers individual consultation to college hopefuls, billing as much as $40,000 per applicant. To give you an idea of what $40,000 can buy:

> [Michele Hernandez] selects classes for students, reviews their homework, and prods them to make an impression on teachers. She checks on the students' grades, scores, rankings. She tells parents when to hire tutors and then makes sure the kids do the extra work. She vets their vacation schedules. She plans their summers. And through it all, she is always available to contend with the college angst that can consume whole families. (Berfield & Tergesen, 2007)

All of this consultant's work is meant to be completely invisible. Regardless of how many drafts of an applicant's admissions essay she may review, she works painstakingly hard to ensure that no one can tell she assisted. It is this invisibility that gives students power with their prospective institution. After her work, the students look like well-rounded, sophisticated individuals worthy of access to the most elite institutions (Berfield & Tergesen, 2007).

With the advent of this consultation field, some admissions representatives have become quite suspicious. One admissions officer at Vanderbilt University stated, "I've read a lot of essays, and I know what a high school student sounds like. . . . When a file feels like it was written by a 45-year-old attorney, it proba-

bly was" (Schouten, 2003). However, what is an admissions officer to do? There are brilliant high school students who can write amazing admissions essays, but there is no way to tell these students apart. Therefore, schools admit students who had their admissions essays written by consultants alongside those admitted on merit.

ACCESS AND SUCCESS

Throughout much of the 20th century and into the 21st, college enrollment in the United States has grown rapidly. In 1972, 9,214,860 individuals were enrolled in postsecondary education. By 2008, that number had risen to 19,102,814, a 107% increase (Snyder & Dillow, 2010) (see Figure 6.4). True, the overall U.S. population had grown in this same period, but only by 45% (U.S. Census Bureau, n.d.).

Communities of color have been a part of the growth of higher education. However, since the United States has a long history of discrimination, any increase for people of color was accompanied by an equal or greater increase for Whites, as shown in Figure 6.5.

From 1972 to 2008, Whites saw their proportion of college enrollment for 18- to 24-year-olds grow 17%. The growth for Blacks was 13.8%, and for Hispanics 12.4%, in that same period (Snyder & Dillow, 2010). Figure 6.6 depicts how these percentages create the present-day complexion of U.S. higher education institutions.

In examining the breadth of these statistics, we can understand the reach of higher education. In 2009, the 18-and-over U.S. population was 226,973,000. Subtracting the 80,699,000 individuals who already have a degree from a postsecondary institution (U.S. Census Bureau, 2009) leaves 146,274,000 people. In that same year, 19,102,814 individuals enrolled in postsecondary education (Snyder & Dillow, 2010). Taking all those pursuing a degree in higher education as a percentage of the total 18-and-over population without a higher education degree puts the percentage of the U.S. adult population pursuing a college degree in 2009 at 13.6%. If we leave in the equation those who already have a degree, because one degree is often still not enough, that enrollment rate drops to 8.4%.

These statistics help us understand the overall small percentage of adults who are accessing higher

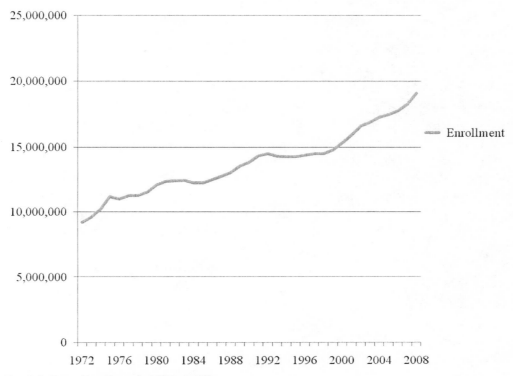

Figure 6.4 Total College Enrollment, 1972–2008

(Snyder & Dillow, 2010)

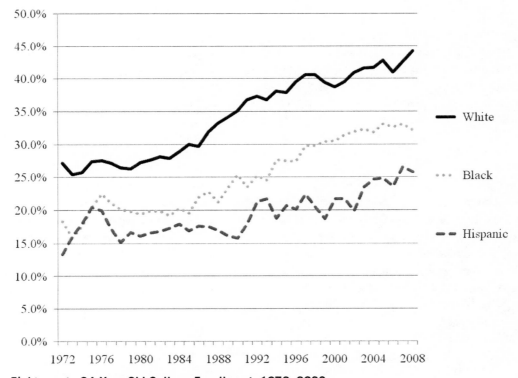

Figure 6.5 Eighteen- to 24-Year-Old College Enrollment, 1972–2008

(Snyder & Dillow, 2010)

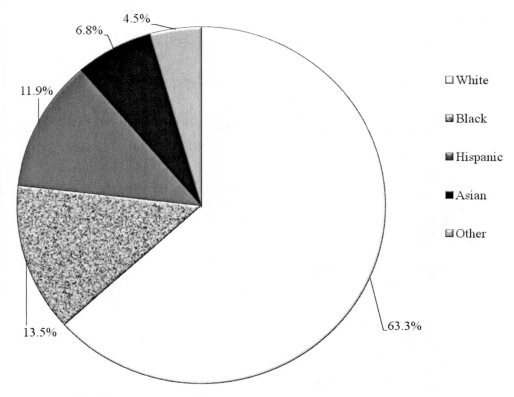

Figure 6.6   College Enrollment by Race, 2008

(Snyder & Dillow, 2010)

education. As to the racial makeup of that group, the percentage of those admitted into higher education in Black and Hispanic communities is only slightly below their representation of the 18-and-over U.S. population (U.S. Census Bureau, 2010). However, we must question this access percentage in two ways. First, where exactly are different communities gaining this access? Second, is this access translating into a degree?

In answering the first question, we must grapple with the unfortunate reality that all higher education institutions were not created equal. Geography, mission, funding, accessibility, admissions criteria, acceptance rate, and a whole host of competing factors that determine prestige separate colleges and universities. While a degree from any college is valuable, my bachelor's degree from Eastern Illinois University, while it is a fine institution, is not worth as much as the same degree from Harvard University. Being an elite, Ivy League institution, Harvard has a reputation and status that garners power for its graduates.

Being able to document the prestige of an institution is a controversial topic, and the *U.S. News & World Report* is often at the center of the storm. Their yearly publication of the "Best Colleges" across the United States centralizes the ranking of academic institutions. While many have serious misgivings about such rankings, the publication does shape the outlook on academia and, therefore, requires attention.

The 2010 *U.S. News & World Report's Ultimate College Guide* provides a ranking of the most selective higher education institutions. These schools have the highest number of applications and subsequent rejections. This creates the assumption that if this many students wish to attend a school and cannot, the education that school provides must be the most valuable. Notwithstanding this specious reasoning, the top 10 institutions from this list are many of the most prestigious schools in the United States. Figure 6.7 lists these institutions in rank order from left to right. The bar graph displays the percentage of Black and Hispanic enrollment in these schools in fall 2008 (U.S. News & World Report, 2009), and the dashed lines indicate the actual

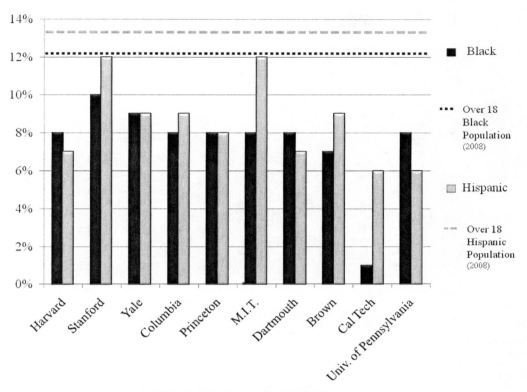

Figure 6.7   U.S. News & World Report 2010, Most Selective Institutions

(U.S. Census Bureau, 2010; U.S. News & World Report, 2009)

percentage of the 18-and-over population for Blacks and Hispanics (U.S. Census Bureau, 2010). As one can see, every single institution falls below the actual community's size within the greater population.

Please note, for the 10 most selective schools the United States has to offer, every single one of them is a private institution. Another part of access is cost, and private institutions carry a huge price tag, many in excess of $50,000 per year.

If students of color generally are not attending these elite institutions, where are they enrolled? To find that answer, one needs only to look lower on the academic hierarchy scale. Community colleges can serve an important function for students seeking entry into academia. These two-year institutions provide access, allowing students to earn credits to transfer to four-year institutions. Such academic work is laudable, but not as valued in the academic community. Since by definition, community colleges largely serve those residing within their community, and since the majority of these institutions have open admissions, it is not easy to find a suitable group to compare against the elite institutions.

Therefore, I have collected demographic data for the 10 largest community colleges in the United States (National Center for Education Statistics [NCES], 2007), ranked in order from left to right in Figure 6.8. The bars contain the information for Black and Hispanic enrollment in fall 2009 (NCES, n.d.), and the dashed lines indicate the actual representation of these communities in the 18-and-over population in the United States (U.S. Census Bureau, 2010).

As one can see, every single community college has at least either Black or Hispanic students outpacing their actual representation in the United States. In five of these institutions, it is both communities. Furthermore, completing course work at a community college does not necessarily lead to a bachelor's degree. The Beginning Postsecondary Students Longitudinal Study followed cohorts of graduating high school students. One cohort of 12,000 students began in 1996, and researchers followed up with the same group again in 1998 and 2001. For the students in this group who entered community college, only 28.9% transferred to a four-year institution (NCES, 2003).

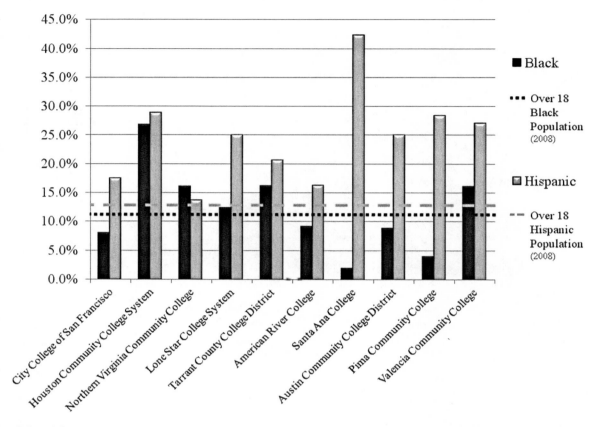

Figure 6.8   U.S. Largest Community Colleges

(NCES, n.d.; U.S. Census Bureau, 2010)

One other segment of higher education deserves reflection—for-profit education. These institutions differ from public and not-for-profit private schools, like Harvard and Yale, by seeking to make a profit for their owners and stockholders from educating college students. Even though public and not-for-profit colleges and universities can be expensive, by law, any surplus money must be channeled back into the institution. According to the U.S. Department of Education, only 364,000 students were enrolled in for-profit institutions in 1998. Ten years later, for-profit enrollment neared 1.5 million (Messer, 2010). Schools like the University of Phoenix have dominated this sector, and many questions have been raised about the value of the education offered at such institutions. Nonetheless, one cannot argue with their reach. However, since for-profit schools are not as forthcoming with their institutional data, I was only able to obtain the demographics for the two largest for-profit systems. First, the University of Phoenix (2009) touts that

30% of its institution is comprised of Black students. Second, Strayer University states that 55.9% of its student population in fall 2009 was Black students (NCES, n.d.).

Even though students are graduating from these institutions, many worry about the viability of a degree paid for in hard-earned dollars. Students enrolled at one for-profit school, Illinois School of Health Careers, discovered the degrees earned at this institution were useless because the Illinois Department of Public Health did not approve its academic program (Dizikes, 2010). Students are in such predicaments all over the country, holding degrees that cannot land them a job, ultimately leading to one in five graduates of for-profit schools defaulting on their student loans (Associated Press, 2009). With approximately 25% of all federal financial aid going into the pockets of these for-profit institutions, this area has come under intense scrutiny (Associated Press, 2010).

The Government Accountability Office (GAO) released a report in August 2010 detailing an investigation into for-profit schools. This organization sent four undercover applicants into 15 for-profit schools around the country and found that all 15 institutions use misleading practices. School representatives lied to applicants about accreditation, degree completion rates, program completion time, and program costs. When it came to financial aid, some applicants were not allowed to talk to an aid representative until they signed an attendance contract. Four of these institutions took further steps by encouraging students to commit fraud. One undercover applicant was told to lie on the Free Application for Federal Student Aid (FAFSA) form about $250,000 the applicant had in the bank. Another representative instructed an applicant to invent children to increase the applicant's federal Pell grant. The undercover applicants wore video recording devices when speaking with admissions representatives; these videos can be accessed on GAO's website (GAO, 2010).

Given all of this information, access does not translate into equity. While the statistics presented document the problem, we miss the scope of this issue by not also highlighting total enrollments, because not only are the elite institutions enrolling a lower percentage of students of color, they also are much smaller institutions. A part of their elitism is the scarcity of their degrees. Community colleges and the for-profit sector, on the other hand, are huge institutions that are churning students through at exponential rates. Figure 6.9 calculates the total enrollments in fall 2009 for the 10 most selective institutions, the 10 largest community colleges, and the data for the University of Phoenix by itself (NCES, n.d.).

Remarkably, while the University of Phoenix is bigger than the 10 largest community colleges put together, 380,232 of its students are in its online programs (NCES, n.d.). These students may never step onto a higher education campus in pursuit of a degree. While these students should be applauded for working

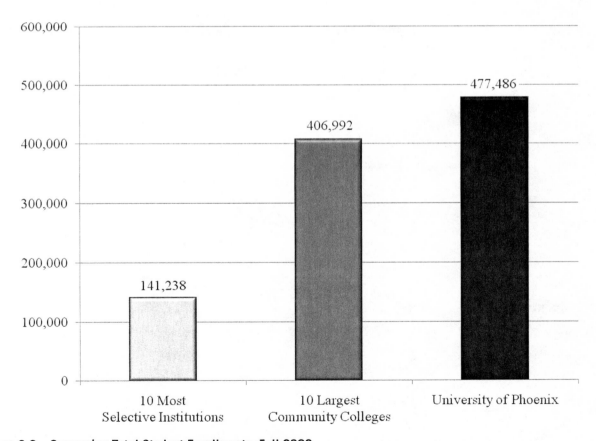

Figure 6.9   Comparing Total Student Enrollments, Fall 2009

(NCES, n.d.)

diligently and trying to improve their life through education, they are not on an even playing field when roughly a third as many students are soaking up lush green lawns and ivy-covered buildings in pursuit of a piece of paper that will be worth more money when hung on a wall.

This question of where students are gaining access is only half the equation. It is vital now that we turn our attention to success. In 1940, 4.6% of the population had a college degree, and that proportion swelled to 29.5% in 2009 (U.S. Census Bureau, 2009), as illustrated in Figure 6.10. These data include all degrees (e.g., bachelor's, master's, doctorate).

The 2009 percentages represent the more than 80 million individuals who had some type of a degree from a postsecondary institution. However, there is racial disparity within this community. Figures 6.11, 6.12, and 6.13 depict the racial communities that have as a highest degree earned a bachelor's degree, master's degree, and doctorate, respectively.

These figures reveal that while we do have increased access, the pipeline through higher education has significant and inequitable leaks. The enrollment num-

bers for Hispanics were reported at 11.9%, but only 6.6% have a bachelor's degree. Black higher education enrollment was 13.5%, but only a rate of 7.6% for having a bachelor's degree. These statistics illustrate that in far too many cases, higher education institutions enroll students and take their money and time, but the end result is not a degree.

CONCLUSION

This chapter provided an overview of the facts and stats regarding access and success for student communities in higher education. It is incredibly important to be well versed in this information, but it is inherently incomplete. Higher education is a culture and, as such, the barriers to success cannot be understood solely through data. The stories of our students must be solicited, listened to, and understood.

Our students' stories would convey the difficult struggle students of color endure in higher education. Making sense of the college culture with little to no assistance is daunting. Even if students overcome that

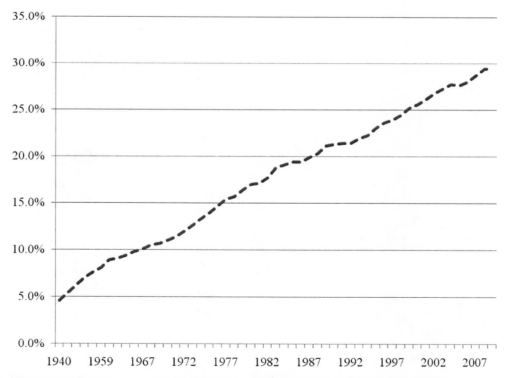

Figure 6.10   Completed Four Years or More of College, 25 Years Old and Over, 1940–2009

(U.S. Census Bureau, 2009)

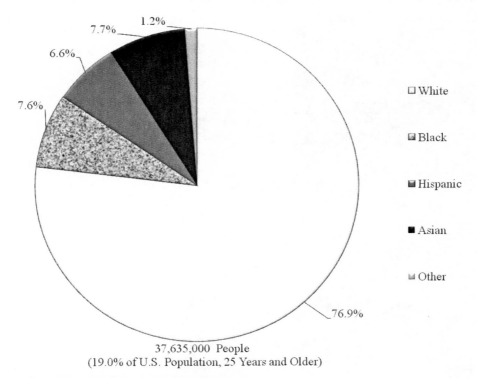

Figure 6.11   Highest Degree Earned, Bachelor's Degree

(U.S. Census Bureau, 2009)

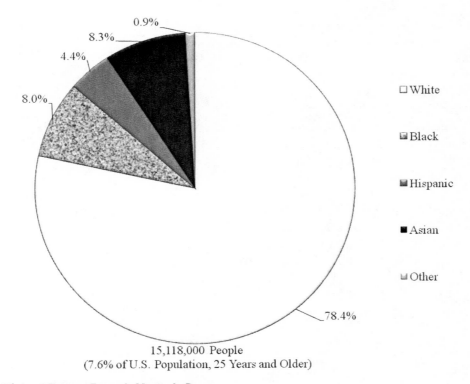

Figure 6.12   Highest Degree Earned, Master's Degree

(U.S. Census Bureau, 2009)

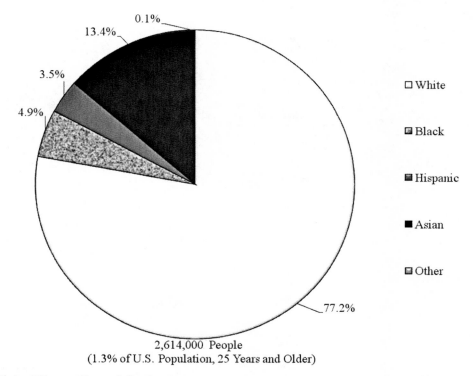

Figure 6.13   Highest Degree Earned, Doctorate

(U.S. Census Bureau, 2009)

hurdle, a new set of challenges emerges. Six months after graduation, students must begin to pay back their student loans. Given that Black and Hispanic college students disproportionately receive financial aid to attend community colleges, while White students are more likely to take aid to attend more elite, private institutions, what is their differential earning potential? Sadly, not all higher education institutions were created equally, and a degree from Harold Washington City College in Chicago is not equal to one from Northwestern University. Additionally, Black and Latino students are often starting with a lower SES than their White counterparts. When they do graduate, the weight of student loan debt is much heavier because of their lower baseline social capital and lower income potential (Orfield, 1992; St. John, 2000). This leads to the question, what does *success* cost in the United States and is that cost just?

REFERENCES

Associated Press. (2009, December 14). For-profit schools hit by loan defaults. *Washington Post*. Retrieved from http://www.washingtontimes.com/news/2009/dec/14/for-profit-schools-hit-by-loan-defaults/

Associated Press. (2010). Ahead of the bell: Senate examines for-profit ed. *Bloomberg Businessweek*. Retrieved from http://www.businessweek.com/ap/financialnews/D9GHL08O0.htm

Ballantine, J. H., & Roberts, K. A. (2009). *Our social world: Condensed version*. Thousand Oaks, CA: Pine Forge Press.

Baum, S., Payea, K., & Steele, P. (2006). *Education pays: Second update*. Washington, DC: College Board.

Berfield S., & Tergesen, A. (2007, October 22). I can get your kid into an Ivy. *Business Week*. Retrieved from http://www.businessweek.com/magazine/content/07_43/b4055063.htm

Bick, J. (2008, September 14). Navigators for the college bound. *New York Times*, 11.

Boccela, K. (2007, October 28). College consultants: Price of admission; more parents pay to give applicants an edge. *Philadelphia Inquirer*, A01.

Cheeseman Day, J., & Newburger, E. C. (2002, July). The big payoff: Educational attainment and synthetic estimates of work-life earnings. *U.S. Department of Commerce*. Retrieved from http://www.census.gov/prod/2002pubs/p23–210.pdf

Next Steps for the Reader

- Regardless of whether you have taken it before, sign up for the SAT. When you receive your score, write a short reflection on your experience taking this assessment, the score you received in comparison to your previous score (if applicable), and what you think this test score means given where you are now in life. Share this reflection with those closest to you to start a conversation about such assessments.
- Identify the community college and university closest to your home. Take a tour of these institutions, looking specifically at computer labs, library materials, classrooms, and community space. Are there any differences in amenities? Additionally, compare those schools' admission acceptance rates, racial demographics, and graduation rates disaggregated by race. If you have a degree from a higher education institution, collect and compare the same data from your alma mater.

Additional Resources for Up-to-Date Facts and Stats

College Board
- Higher Education Research—http://professionals.collegeboard.com/data-reports-research/cb/higher-ed
- Higher Education Trends & Related Reports—http://professionals.collegeboard.com/data-reports-research/trends
- Race, Ethnicity, and Socioeconomic Status—http://professionals.collegeboard.com/data-reports-research/cb/race

Color and Money: How Rich White Kids Are Winning the War over College Affirmative Action Blog
- Main website—http://www.colorandmoney.blogspot.com/

Institute for Higher Education Policy
- Homepage—http://www.ihep.org/
- Access and Success—http://www.ihep.org/Research/access-success.cfm
- Diversity—http://www.ihep.org/Research/diversity.cfm

Pathways to College Network
- Homepage—http://www.pathwaystocollege.net
- College Access and Success State Data—http://www.pathwaystocollege.net/statelibraries/AllStates.aspx

National Center for Education Statistics
- Beginning Postsecondary Students Longitudinal Study—http://nces.ed.gov/surveys/bps/
- Digest of Education Statistics—http://nces.ed.gov/programs/digest/index.asp
- National Postsecondary Education Cooperative—http://nces.ed.gov/npec/

U.S. Census Bureau
- Higher Education: Degrees—http://www.census.gov/compendia/statab/cats/education/higher_education_degrees.html

College Board. (2009). *2009 college bound seniors: Total group profile report.* New York: The College Board.

Dizikes, C. (2010, June 24). A lesson they won't forget: For-profit school's error costs students certification. *Chicago Tribune.* Retrieved from http://www.chicagotribune.com/news/education/ct-met-for-profit-schools-20100622,0,3297701

Fluehr-Lobban, C. (2006). *Race and racism: An introduction.* Lanham, MD: AltaMira Press.

Foner, E. (1997). Hiring quotas for White males only. In R. Delgado & J. Stefancic (Eds.), *Critical White studies: Looking behind the mirror* (pp. 24–26). Philadelphia, PA: Temple University Press.

Freedman, S. G. (2006, April 26). In college entrance frenzy, a lesson out of left field. *New York Times,* 9.

Government Accountability Office (GAO). (2010, August 4). *For-profit colleges: Undercover testing finds colleges encouraged fraud and engaged in deceptive and questionable marketing practices.* (Publication No. GAO-10–948T). Retrieved from http://www.gao.gov/new.items/d10948t.pdf

Gratz v. Bollinger, 539 U.S. 244 (2003).

Grutter v. Bollinger, 539 U.S. 306 (2003).

Hoover, E. (2011, February 17). DePaul becomes biggest private university to go "test optional." *Chronicle of Higher Education.* Retrieved from http://chronicle.com/article/DePaul-U-Will-Make-SAT-and/126396/

Jencks, C. (1998). Racial bias in testing. In. C. Jencks & M. Phillips (Eds.), *The black-white test score gap* (pp. 55–85). Washington, DC: Brookings Institution Press.

Kane, T. J. (1998). Racial and ethnic preferences in college admissions. In. C. Jencks & M. Phillips (Eds.), *The black-white test score gap* (pp. 431–456). Washington, DC: Brookings Institution Press.

Karabel, J. (2006). *The chosen: The hidden history of admission and exclusion at Harvard, Yale, and Princeton.* New York: Mariner Books.

Katz, S., Lautenschlager, G. J., Blackburn, A. B., & Harris, F. H. (1990). Answering reading comprehension items without passages on the SAT. *Psychological Science, 1*(2), 122–127.

Katznelson, I. (2005). *When affirmative action was White: An untold history of racial inequality in twentieth-century America.* New York: W. W. Norton.

Kidder, W. C., & Rosner, J. (2002–2003). How the SAT creates "built-in headwinds": An educational and legal analysis of disparate impact. *Santa Clara Law Review, 43,* 131–211.

Messer, J. (2010, June 24). Harkin starts hearings on for-profit colleges today. *Daily Iowan.* Retrieved from http://www.dailyiowan.com/2010/06/24/Metro/17675.html

Micceri, T. (2007). *How we justify and maintain White, male academic status quo through the use of biased college admissions requirements.* Tampa, FL: University of South Florida, Office of the Provost.

National Center for Education Statistics (NCES). (n.d.) *Search for schools, colleges, and libraries.* Retrieved from http://nces.ed.gov/globallocator/

National Center for Education Statistics (NCES). (2003). *Student effort and educational progress: Postsecondary persistence and progress.* Retrieved from http://nces.ed.gov/programs/coe/2003/section3/indicator19.asp#info

National Center for Education Statistics (NCES). (2007). *Enrollment of the 120 largest degree-granting college and university campuses, by selected characteristics and institution: Fall 2007.* Retrieved from http://nces.ed.gov/programs/digest/d09/tables/dt09_235.asp

Orfield, G. (1992, Fall). Money, equity, and college access. *Harvard Educational Review, 62*(3), 337–372.

Padilla, A. M., & Borsato, G. N. (2008). Issues in culturally appropriate psychoeducational assessment. In L. A. Suzuki & J. G. Ponterotto (Eds.), *Handbook of multicultural assessment: Clinical, psychological, and educational applications* (3rd ed.) (pp. 5–21). San Francisco: John Wiley.

Pathways to College Network. (2003). *A shared agenda: A leadership challenge to improve college access and success.* Retrieved from http://www.pathwaystocollege.net/pdf/sharedagenda_FullReport.pdf

Schmidt, P. (2007). *Color and money: How rich white kids are winning the war over college affirmative action.* New York: Palgrave Macmillan.

Schouten, F. (2003, April 29). More parents are hiring pros to coach kids for admission. *USA Today.* Retrieved from http://www.usatoday.com/news/nation/2003-04-29-hired-usat_x.htm

Shapira, I. (2007, August 5). More are taking a rain check on college. *Washington Post,* C01.

Snyder, T. D., & Dillow, S. A. (2010). *Digest of Education Statistics 2009.* Washington, DC: National Center for Education Statistics, Institute of Education Sciences, U.S. Department of Education.

St. Clair, S., & Cohen, J. S. (2009, June 2). U. of I. clout list put on suspension: University of Illinois appoints panel to review admissions. *Chicago Tribune.* Retrieved from http://www.chicagotribune.com/news/local/chi-college-clout-02-jun02,0,7886322.story

St. Clair, S., Cohen, J. S. & Becker, R. (2009, May 31). U. of I. admissions: How politicians pressured university to admit students. *Chicago Tribune.* Retrieved from http://www.chicagotribune.com/news/local/chi-college-clout-31-may 31,0,7230960.story

St. John, E. P. (2000). The impact of student aid on recruitment and retention: What the research indicates. In M. D. Coomes (Ed.), *The role student aid plays in enrollment management* (pp. 61–75). San Francisco: Jossey-Bass.

Steele, C. M., & Aronson, J. (1998). Stereotype threat and the test performance of academically successful African Americans. In. C. Jencks & M. Phillips (Eds.), *The black-white test score gap* (pp. 401–427). Washington, DC: Brookings Institution Press.

Steinberg, J. (2011, March 16). SAT's reality TV essay stumps some. *New York Times,* p. A20.

Turner, R. (1990). *The past and future of affirmative action: A guide and analysis for human resource professionals and corporate counsel.* New York: Quorum Books.

University of Michigan. (2003, February 19). *Q&A re University of Michigan former admissions policies.* Retrieved from http://www.vpcomm.umich.edu/admissions/archivedocs/q&a.html

University of Phoenix. (2009). *Academic annual report.* Retrieved from http://www.phoenix.edu/about_us/publications/academic-annual-report.html

U.S. Bureau of Labor Statistics. (2010, September 3). Table A-4: Employment status of the civilian population 25 years and over by educational attainment. Retrieved from http://www.bls.gov/news.release/empsit.t04.htm

U.S. Census Bureau. (n.d.). *International database.* Retrieved from http://www.census.gov/ipc/www/idb/country.php

U.S. Census Bureau. (2009). *Educational attainment in the United States: 2009.* Retrieved from http://www.census.gov/population/www/socdemo/education/cps2009.html

U.S. Census Bureau. (2010). *The 2010 statistical abstract.* Retrieved from http://www.census.gov/compendia/statab/

U.S. News & World Report. (2009). *Ultimate college guide: 2010* (7th ed.). Naperville, IL: Sourcebooks, Inc.

Whiston, S. C. (2009). *Principles and applications of assessment in counseling* (3rd ed.). Belmont, CA: Brooks/Cole, Cengage Learning.

7

Next Steps as a Social Change Agent

It is easier to build strong children than to repair broken [women and] men.

FREDERICK DOUGLASS

THIS FREDERICK DOUGLASS QUOTATION SUMS UP the primary purpose of this entire text. It is far easier to fix the systemic racism problems of children than it is for adults. That is why our work as social change agents must begin today, even though we will definitely encounter resistance. This final chapter outlines two common defense mechanisms often triggered in the face of change as well as a tool to help envision our role as a social change agent.

DEFENDING THE STATUS QUO

The individual facts and stats found in this book do not stand alone. Every detail is part of a greater whole, feeding and sustaining a well-developed system in which children of color experience discrimination. Accepting this truth counters a long-standing, deeply ingrained belief system—meritocracy. Meritocracy is the notion that success is a product of an individual's hard work, and this idea is central to the narrative of the American Dream. This narrative teaches that if people simply "pull themselves up by their bootstraps" they will garner greater societal rewards. While I fully support individuals working hard and performing to the very best of their abilities, this ideology fails to account for the numerous factors that significantly affect individual success. As exemplified throughout this book, racism is in every facet of life and simply believing in meritocracy will not change this reality. Meri-

tocracy does not acknowledge this fact because to do so would prove this belief system to be a fairy tale. Letting go of the myth of meritocracy is incredibly difficult, even stressful. When we challenge people to accept a new concept of self and society, many use defense mechanisms, which protect people psychologically from having their worldview challenged. There are two commonly used mechanisms in these dialogues. First, those wishing to dismiss this book's Color by Number game may employ the rhetoric of individual responsibility. Second, when the individual responsibility argument fails, people distance themselves from the problem, creating a mind-set in which they share no responsibility for creating positive social change.

As for the first defense mechanism, statements such as, "Well, if *they* just worked harder, *they* could achieve too," are often made. Such a statement serves two purposes. First, it puts the onus of responsibility on the disenfranchised, in this case children of color. However, what work can children of color perform that will improve their asthma, for example? Second, focusing on individual responsibility takes away any personal accountability the speaker might have for benefiting from the status quo. Yet, privileged group members do collectively benefit because we are not merely individuals; we are a society sharing a history that was shaped by racism. Social justice educators often use an analogy to exemplify how history informs present-day societal issues; it involves the game of MONOPOLY.

Imagine for a moment you and I are playing a game of MONOPOLY, and for the first half of the game I am cheating in every way imaginable. I control the entire scope of real estate holdings and prohibit you from owning property other than Baltic and Vermont avenues. I am also in charge of the bank and refuse to give you the same money I am allotted at the start of the game. Furthermore, you can simply forget about collecting your $200 when you pass Go; I may bequeath you $50 if I am feeling generous. When you land in jail, you are neither allowed to pay or roll for your freedom; you remain held until I deem it necessary for you to be released. While you are in jail and suspended from expanding your MONOPOLY fortune, I am busy "working hard" to acquire property, soaking up the gainful opportunities found in the railroads and utilities, all while accumulating as much cash as I can.

As this inequitable treatment continues, your grumbling turns to complaining and finally to outright protest. This protest creates a demand for change, a demand I attempt to ignore, but ultimately cannot. You demand the right to own any property you wish. I concede. You demand to have the same rules when passing Go. I relent. You demand equitable regulations during time spent in jail. I yield. We agree to play by the rules of fundamental fairness from this moment forward. The playing field is now leveled and each of us now begins to "work hard" to acquire a fortune. However, we are not restarting the game. We will continue playing the same game, in which I retain all the money, property, housing, railroads, utilities, and Get Out of Jail Free cards I "earned" during the first half of the game.

What chances do you have of *ever* winning this game? I own the majority of the board, including the most valuable and attractive properties. I have put hotels on much of my real estate to increase my profit margin, and I have plenty of cash tucked away for whatever twists and turns lie ahead. You, on the other hand, live on Baltic Avenue.

The statistics comprising this book are born from a racist past. This past constructs our society, shapes our individual experiences, and supports the impediments to advancement for people of color in general and children of color in specific. Yet, we hide behind the guise of fair play, equality, and the broken individualistic ideology of the American Dream. We pretend where people sit in life is a function of their work ethic, and we do not take into account that they were born into a system with a marred history. We owe more to our children than placing the blame for their circumstances at their feet.

If we are successful in breaking through the individualism rhetoric, there is yet one more defense mechanism to overcome. This final hurdle is diffusion of responsibility; this is the phenomenon whereby people feel less personal responsibility to become involved when they are part of a large group. Roy Baumeister and Brad Bushman (2008) detail this entity well:

> With several potential helpers around, the personal responsibility of each bystander is reduced. If you are only one person present, 100% of the responsibility for providing help rests on your shoulders; if two people are present, each has 50% responsibility; if four people are present, each has 25% responsibility, and so on. In crowds, people think, "Perhaps someone else will help; perhaps someone else has already called for help." With everyone thinking that someone else will help or has helped, nobody helps. (p. 280)

Another name for this phenomenon is the bystander effect. These entities are so powerful the Red Cross takes heed of them in CPR training. The Red Cross teaches trainees to point to a specific person to call 911 after they have checked the scene and the victim. Calling out one person is crucial because if you call to a crowd, you may simply receive blank stares even though crowd members are thinking, "Wow, I hope somebody calls 911 to help that person!" However, in pointing at an individual, you have clearly cast the responsibility upon someone.

Casting responsibility in this Color by Number game is difficult, if not impossible. Each of us comprises such a small fraction of life in the United States that we do not feel culpable for the plight of another. It is far easier to assume this is someone else's problem. In a nation of more than 300 million people, it is easy to spread responsibility so thinly over everyone that, ultimately, nothing is done. There is an applicable social justice truth that has experienced many iterations: "For evil in the world to prosper it does not require good people to participate, only that they remain silent." This is the state of affairs in the health-care industry, environmental protection, the juvenile justice system, and every level of education; the silence is deafening.

In combating this diffusion of responsibility, it is vital to conceptualize concretely how this work can be done, how change can happen. This takes us into the final phase of this book where we develop an action plan for the future.

WORKING AS A SOCIAL CHANGE AGENT

I intended this book to be a reference tool for social change agents who are teaching and learning about antiracism. Agents of social change must be armed with the facts and stats that support this movement. There are well-developed systems in place to thwart our attempts at creating change. We cannot afford to leave anything to chance, and while I believe that the stories and experiences of people of color must not be forgotten, there are times when knowing the correct fact or stat will be the tipping point in creating real and lasting change.

However, in looking at this work, everyone from the social justice veteran to the burgeoning antiracism activist can have difficulty envisioning her or his role in creating change. Social justice issues are widespread and envelope all of our lives. Where does the work begin? Where will the most impact be felt? In the life of any social change agent, there are times where the direction forward is unclear. The swirling questions can become a "paralysis by analysis" whereby we become overwhelmed by potential options and tactics. Then, without knowing the absolute right path, we can become stagnant. It is important to know that there are practical mechanisms to use as you attempt to create social change.

The facts and stats on every page of this text describe an overarching, deeply entrenched system. This macro-level view is necessary for us to understand the reach of racism. However, our work doesn't have to begin at this macro-level; too few of us have the actual power and influence to create large-scale change on our own. Focusing on far-reaching endeavors, while laudable, may frustrate even the most talented and committed social change agent. This frustration may rob a person of an opportunity to make a positive impact. The following story from an unknown monk in 1100 C.E. illuminates this point.

When I was a young man, I wanted to change the world. I found it was difficult to change the world, so I tried to change my nation. When I found I couldn't change the nation, I began to focus on my town. I couldn't change the town and as an older man, I tried to change my family. Now, as an old man, I realize the only thing I can change is myself, and suddenly I realize that if long ago I had changed myself, I could have made an impact on my family. My family and I could have made an impact on our town. Their impact could have changed the nation and I could have indeed changed the world. (as quoted in Workman, 2009, p. 106)

We all have different levels of influence within our lives. Like the parable denotes, those entities closest to us are the best opportunities we have at educating and developing a social justice mind-set. We see these people daily, know them intimately, and have the trust built to start uncomfortable conversations on difficult topics such as race and racism. On a national or global level, we have little ability to create real and lasting change as one person. To conceptualize these differing levels of influence, some educators employ a concentric circle diagram, as depicted in Figure 7.1.

This figure illustrates the varying spheres of influences within a person's life. At the center of the figure is the entity where the most influence can be leveraged— you, the social change agent. You never complete learning, living, talking, developing, and exploring, the demanding emotional work needed to be effective in your role. The world changes every day and your personal development must continue to keep up.

The next level of influence is your family and friends. The foundation built with these groups will allow you to enter into stressful conversations. Hearing the difficult truths found in this book is easier when the words are spoken by someone who loves us. You can tell your family and friends that you have no agenda other than the love and respect you have for them. You are simply challenging them to be the people you know they are. It may be that you are the first person ever to talk to them about race and racism free from the angst and judgment such conversations may be clouded by elsewhere.

From here, we get to the next sphere, our places of employment, coworkers, and neighborhoods. Certainly, you have a measure of influence here, raising

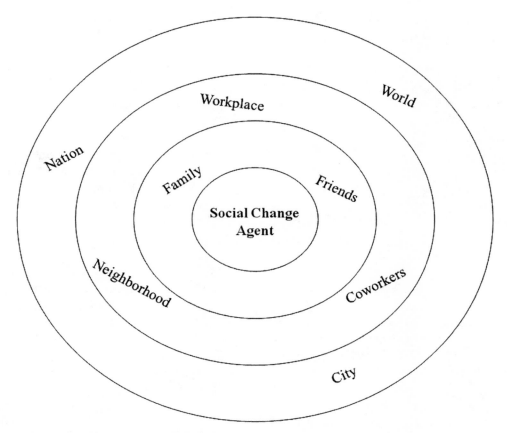

Figure 7.1   Spheres of Influence as a Social Change Agent

conversations, seeking input from those who are silenced, and offering equitable and just solutions to problems that arise. But, into the workplace, many of us are not the boss. However, even if you are, every boss has another boss, pushing the ultimate power to create change a level higher. This reality does not mean you are powerless. It is important to devote your energy to the specific areas where you can have a positive impact and put forth your best effort on those endeavors. If we all did that, the sum would become much greater due to our individual parts.

Finally, there is your city, country, and the entirety of the world. As a single person you have very little influence on these levels on a day-to-day basis. The single greatest tool at your disposal to affect these levels is your opportunity to vote, a privilege not everyone enjoys. It is your duty to question and investigate candidates and proposed legislation. Simply voting with one political party lets politicians off much too easy; they should earn your vote every single time.

Figure 7.1 does resonate with me, but it is a flawed representation since the world's problems are depicted as revolving around the social change agent and the agent stands alone. This is an inaccurate portrayal of social justice work. In collaboration with Vijay Pendakur, we developed an alternative tool, which can be found in Figure 7.2.

In Figure 7.2, the varying levels do not encircle the social change agent, but rather, they branch out, becoming more difficult to influence at each level. Of greater importance, Figure 7.2 illustrates that no social change agent is alone in this movement; every icon on the left side of the figure represents the greater community of social justice educators and activists who are always there for support.

Community is incredibly important in this work. Too often, social change agents concentrate exclusively on what they alone stand for. However, this is only half of the equation. I personally challenge every reader to be accountable not only for asserting *what*

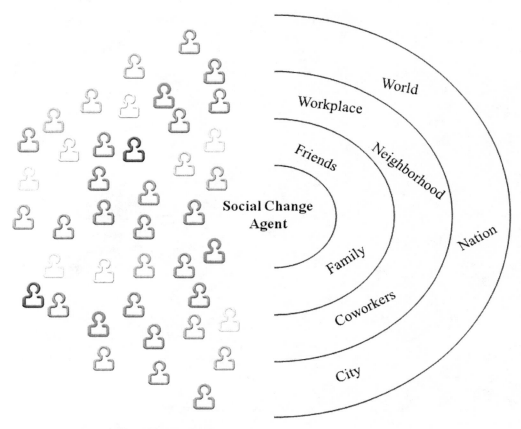

Figure 7.2 Levels of Influence as a Social Change Agent

you stand for, but also, *whom you stand with*. Any social change agent working alone, without the challenge and support of community, will ultimately be ineffective. Social justice solely envisioned by an individual is a failure.

When we think of the great leaders of social change throughout history, often we too narrowly attribute their success to them personally. In doing so, we ignore the role community played every step of the way. The most apt example in a book on the plight of racism is Dr. Martin Luther King Jr. Dr. King led a revolution that fundamentally changed this country. To truly understand Dr. King as a social change agent, Figure 7.2 must be augmented in two ways. Therefore, we offer Figure 7.3 as an individual conceptualization of Dr. King's levels of influence.

In Figure 7.3 the varying levels of influence in Dr. King's life are compressed. In his work he had a profound ability to influence the levels farthest from him, and many may wrongly assume this stemmed from

Dr. King himself. It did not. His incredible influence came from the other change in Figure 7.3, the gigantic and vibrant community he stood with during the movement for civil rights.

In this culture, those we identify as leaders often get too much credit and too much blame for world developments. Giving over such power to these leaders distances us from the struggle and diminishes our personal responsibility for creating change. The March on Washington was not made special by Dr. King's "I Have a Dream" speech; it was made special by the thousands who gathered to listen to those inspiring words. Community, not a speaker at a microphone, is the crucial factor needed to create real and lasting change. As such, in attempting to make the greatest impact on the farthest reaches in your levels of influence, do not focus solely on the obstacles to change *against* you. You must pay attention to the allies standing *with* you and seek to increase the breadth and vitality of those connections. Multiplying and

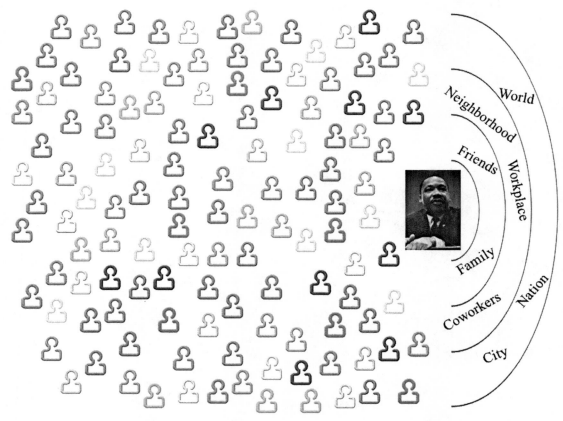

Figure 7.3   Levels of Influence for Dr. Martin Luther King Jr.

(Dr. King photo-Trikosko, 1964)

strengthening the social change agents who comprise your community will make reaching those farthest levels of influence all the more possible.

Use the tools in this book, as well as a host of many others, to talk with those closest to you. Of course, I cannot promise all these conversations will go well nor will you be able to influence every single person in your life. However, the day we believe people lack the ability to develop and learn is the day we have stopped working for justice. I did not understand or believe the incredible reach of racism the first time someone presented it to me. It was only through the patient and persistent dialogue I had with people I trusted that I began to open my heart and mind.

Such dialogues remain crucial in my life because I would never claim I have somehow "arrived." I am forever a work in progress, and any development I achieve is due to my community providing challenge and support. My community is not only those I see in person; it includes people all over the United States and I keep in contact with them via conferences, e-mail, and Face-

book. In an effort to expand community further and offer a space to discuss the topics raised in this text, I have started a Facebook group named after the title of this book. I hope to see dialogue in this group about the triumphs and struggles of social change agents so we may learn from one another and always remember we are not alone.

REFERENCES

Baumeister, R. F., & Bushman, B. J. (2008). *Social psychology & human nature*. Belmont, CA: Wadsworth Publishing.

Trikosko, M. S. (photographer). (1964). Marin Luther King press conference [photograph]. Retrieved from http://www.loc.gov/pictures/item/2003688129.

Workman, N. (2009). Change. In S. R. Komives, W. Wagner, & Associates (Eds.), *Leadership for a better world: Understanding the social change model of leadership development* (pp. 101–143). San Francisco: Jossey-Bass.

About the Author

ART MUNIN IS CURRENTLY DEAN OF STUDENTS AT DePaul University, working extensively with student advocacy, education, wellness, and conduct. In addition, he serves as an adjunct professor at DePaul for the First Year and Counseling Programs and at Loyola University Chicago for the Higher Education program, teaching a course entitled "Social Justice in Higher Education." Art is a practiced and experienced consultant having started his own company in 2004 (www.artmunin.com). In the years since, he has worked with a variety of educational institutions, not-for-profits, and municipalities all over the country by providing workshops and consultation on diversity and justice education, ally development, White privilege, socially just decision making, and leadership.

Though this is Art's first book, he has coauthored chapters in *The Handbook for Student Leadership Development* (2011) and *When "Minorities Are Strongly Encouraged to Apply": Diversity and Affirmative Action in Higher Education* (2009) in addition to other publications. He earned a PhD in higher education and an MEd in community counseling at Loyola University Chicago, an MA in multicultural communication at DePaul University, and a BA in psychology from Eastern Illinois University. Art lives in Chicago with his partner Heidi and dog Rocky. Art and Heidi are expecting twins in June 2012.

Index